W9-CEG-069

TEACHING
THE
VIETNAM WAR

TEACHING
THE
VIETNAM WAR

A Critical Examination of School Texts
and an Interpretive Comparative History
Utilizing The Pentagon Papers and Other Documents

WILLIAM L. GRIFFEN
and JOHN MARCIANO

ALLANHELD, OSMUN   Montclair

Burgess

DS
558.2
.G74
1979

ALLANHELD, OSMUN & CO. PUBLISHERS, INC.
19 Brunswick Road, Montclair, N.J. 07042

Published in the United States of America in 1979
by Allanheld, Osmun & Co.

Library of Congress Cataloging in Publication Data
Griffen, William L
Teaching the Vietnam War.

Bibliography: p.
Includes index.
1. Vietnamese Conflict, 1961-1975—United States—
Text-books. 2. Vietnamese Conflict, 1961-1975—United
States. 3. United States—History—1945- —Text-books.
4. United States—History—1945- I. Marciano,
J. D., joint author. II. Title.
DS558.2.G74   959.704'3373   78-73553
ISBN 0-916672-23-9

Printed in the United States of America

Dedication

In her fine study of what the Vietnam War did to Americans, *Winners and Losers*, Gloria Emerson shares a letter from an American soldier in Vietnam. It was opened, as he instructed, after his death, and his closing plea read, "As I lie dead, please grant my last request. Help me inform the American people, the silent majority who have not yet voiced their opinions." What was it this nineteen-year-old medical corpsman wished to make known? "The war that has taken my life and many thousands before me is immoral, unlawful and an atrocity. . . . I had no choice as to my fate. It was predetermined by the war-mongering hypocrites in Washington."*

Our work speaks to the plea of that silenced soldier and to all the victims, American and Vietnamese, whose courage, suffering, and struggle has marked this epic conflict.

---

*Quoted in Gloria Emerson, *Winners and Losers: Battles, Retreats, Gains, Losses and Ruins from a Long War* (New York: Random House, 1976), p. 101.

Foreword

When history is falsified, it is not simply intellectual error. There are huge practical consequences. For the rulers of any society (that is, those who make and enforce the rules for their own profit and power)—whether in the United States, the Soviet Union, or any other nation-state—it is essential that the majority of people believe in their government. When any population begins to doubt that those in power are acting in the best interests of the people, when they begin to suspect that "national security is in danger!" is a cover-up by corporations and politicians who fear that their own wealth and supremacy are in danger—then the Establishment must move quickly to restore the good name of the government.

The United States government lost its good name during the war in Vietnam—not only in the rest of the world, which watched the cruel bombing of peasant villages (seven million tons of bombs, three times the tonnage dropped on Europe and Asia in World War II), but also among Americans. The war illuminated the whole political landscape, and what the public learned went far beyond what happened in Vietnam—so far beyond as to frighten the Establishment. Many Americans learned that government leaders, whether liberal or conservative, Democrat or Republican, could not be trusted. They began to suspect the most reputable of national institutions—the corporations, the politicians, the FBI and CIA, the military—of moral failure. In the summer of 1975 a Harris Poll showed that over a nine-year period, the public's confidence in the military had dropped from 62% to 29%, in the President and Congress from 42% to 13%, in business from 55% to 18%.

Since 1975, the Establishment has tried strenuously to reestablish the public's confidence in the system. Part of this effort is the retelling of the history of the Vietnam War. It is not that the filmmakers, novelists, and textbook writers are engaged in a giant conspiracy to distort the truth. But with a few exceptions (the film *Coming Home*, the book *Dispatches*), the money made available for films, the acceptability of textbooks by school committees, and the atmosphere of uncritical patriotism nurtured in this country long before the Vietnam War seem to conspire to construct an environment in which the truth is mangled and a whole new generation deceived.

The film *The Deerhunter* was shown in 1979 to tens of millions of Americans. (By contrast, *Hearts and Minds*, a documentary film passionately critical of the Vietnam War, could not find movie theatres willing to show it, and the film company that first authorized it withdrew the financial support needed for advertisement and distribution.) In *The Deerhunter*, the viciousness of the U.S. government's war on the Vietnamese is enveloped and obscured in the innocence of the individual GI's—working-class kids from a town in Pennsylvania—who fought that war.

In the prize-winning novel *Going After Cacciato* by Tim O'Brien, the Establishment's best hope is realized: the war is seen as an honest error, born of good intentions. The main character muses:

Even in Vietnam—wasn't the intent to restrain forces of incivility? The *intent*. Wasn't it to impede tyranny, aggression, repression? To promote some vision of goodness? Oh something had gone terribly wrong. But the aims, the purposes, the ends— weren't they right?

This passage embodies a profoundly important confusion between the ends of the soldiers, and the ends of the corporate-military-political elite that ran the war.

What the film and book industries do to the general public, the textbook industry—aided by school committees closely scrutinized by local politicians—does to youngsters in school. No one has documented this consistent distortion of the Vietnam War in textbooks until this volume of William Griffen and John Marciano. In addition, they give us a concise and accurate history of the Vietnam War against which to measure those texts.

Their accomplishment is rare: they show with compelling evidence that the educational system, far from being "objective," fulfills the aims of the Establishment. Let us hope that their work will stimulate a reexamination of the way history is taught in our schools. Perhaps it can also inspire all of us to insist that the truth be kept straight for our generation and those that follow.

Professor Howard Zinn
Boston University

Contents

Preface

This study was designed to analyze how the Vietnam War
was explained to American students. We selected 28 high-
school textbooks* widely used in social studies and history
courses throughout the country. The majority of these are
sample texts that were acquired by the Teaching Materials
Center at the State University of New York, College at
Cortland. The remainder are texts now being used in central
New York State.

Part I of the study is the *Textbook Synthesis*, a review of
the books to determine what has been written about America's role in the Vietnam War. We divided the war chrono-
logically into three periods: (1) the origins of U.S. involvement; (2) the Diem Era, from the Geneva Agreements in 1954
to Diem's assassination in 1963, and the real emergence of
direct U.S. involvement; (3) the escalation of the war under
President Johnson, Nixon's "Vietnamization" of the war,
and the end of the war. In the *Synthesis* we have attempted
to remain faithful to the substance of the textbooks; therefore
contradictions, distortions and inaccuracies have been left in
their original form, undisturbed by our critical comments.
Quotations from the texts have been woven into the nar-

*See page 3 for a list of the textbooks examined.

rative to capture the actual language of the material. Our critical analysis of the *Textbook Synthesis*, which deals with the contradictions, distortions and inaccuracies, appears in the latter section of Part I and in our history of the war, Part II.

Part II provides a concise history of the Vietnam War, divided into the three periods that correspond to Part I but independent of the textbook histories. We made extensive use of *The Pentagon Papers*, official government reports, and seldom-encountered (at least in the media and the schools) sources that question fundamentally the basic nature of America's Vietnam policy and foreign policy in general. The concluding chapter in Part II discusses the social function of history textbooks within the larger purposes of American education and argues that such texts perform an ideological function: to pass on an uncritical acceptance of the official view of the Vietnam War; in particular, to view the war either as an honorable policy or as a mistake, but not as part of a deliberate policy of imperialism and aggression.

At the beginning of this study, the decision was made to focus exclusively on Vietnam. This in no way denies the crucial relationship of Cambodia and Laos to the Vietnam War. Our decision was based fundamentally on the textbook examination of the war, which is restricted primarily to Vietnam. We have also concerned ourselves with the war itself and not with American reaction to it, except within the textbook discussion. The nature of the Cambodian and Laotian conflicts and the American antiwar movement are each topics that deserve a full and separate treatment, and this was not possible within the context of this study.

Acknowledgments

We wish to thank the following individuals for their assistance and encouragement on this project:

Robert Knowles, who worked closely with us on the early and crucial stages.

Professor Noam Chomsky of M.I.T., Professor Howard Zinn of Boston University, and Jan Barry, Vietnam veteran, and editor of two fine anthologies of poetry on the war, *Demilitarized Zones* and *Winning Hearts and Minds,* for the critical task of reading and commenting on the Vietnam history section of the book. Their criticisms resulted in necessary revisions and, we feel, a much improved work. They responded to "deadline" requests, and their counsel was marked by the same kind of insights that has characterized their writing on the war. Our previous admiration for them has only been deepened by their involvement in this project. We hope that the final effort meets the high standards they have set in their intellectual labors.

Kay Cook, our typing colleague, with the deepest appreciation for "suffering" graciously and in good humor through the many changes that passed through her hands. She has lived with this book for the past few years, and her skills and support have been absolutely essential to its completion.

Sherry Cute, Mary Beth DiBiase, and Kathy Kumpf, for their typing assistance.

Jonathan Kozol, who read parts of the manuscript, for his support and encouragement.

Dik Cool and Chris Murray of the Syracuse Peace Council, for their comments and suggestions on earlier drafts.

Matthew Held, our publisher, for his counsel and faith in this project.

To our loved ones, who understood the importance of this work and the demands it made upon our lives.

Introduction

After every war in which America has fought, history textbooks have interpreted that war to succeeding generations.
Interpretations in the past have always stressed the necessity
of our involvement and defended the correctness and morality of America's wartime role and conduct. Almost without
exception, self-righteous nationalism has been emphasized
at the expense of objective, honest analyses of American
policy.

As early as 1966, the Defense and State departments were
disseminating instant history on the Vietnam War to millions of American students. That year they distributed 1,600
copies of *Why Vietnam?*, a film the noted American historian Henry Steele Commager described thus: "It is not
history. It is not even journalism. It is propaganda, naked
and unashamed." And he warned, "Let us look briefly at this
film, for it is doubtless a kind of dry run of what we will get
increasingly in the future."[1]

Commager's statements are frightening in retrospect: We
have seen this Cold War cascade before, applied almost
universally to different historical situations. The film includes the Munich appeasement analogy, the division of
Vietnam at the 17th parallel into two countries (Free and
Communist), Communist terrorism, Communist aggres-

sion for world domination, and America fulfilling solemn pledges in the free world. The government film is further described by Commager:

Now the scene shifts to Vietnam. In 1954, says our narrator, "the long war is over, and the Communists are moving in." It is a statement which has only the most fortuitous relation to reality. The long war was indeed over—the war between the Vietnamese and the French. But to label the Vietnamese who fought against the French "Communists" and to assume that somehow they "moved in" (they were already there) is a distortion of history.[2]

Even five years before Watergate, Professor Commager could say: "What is needed is a Truth in Packaging Act for the United States government."

The dissemination of *Why Vietnam?* in high schools and colleges is no isolated episode in the manipulation of public opinion by government, but part of a larger pattern. We must view it in connection with the publication program of the USIA, the clandestine activities of the CIA, and the vendetta of the Passport Office against travel to unpopular countries, or by unpopular people, as part of an almost instinctive attempt (we cannot call it anything so formal as a program) to control American thinking about foreign relations. We had supposed, in our innocence, that this sort of thing was the special prerogative of totalitarian governments, but it is clear we were mistaken.[3]

Add to the publication program of the USIA and the Defense and State departments the publication programs of the merged corporate business and textbook industries, and the direction of the next generation's "history" lessons becomes clear.

School textbooks, weekly news readers, and other curricular materials should be examined as to how the Vietnam War and America's foreign policy in that war are reported. Materials characterized by distortions, omissions, and oversimplifications should be so identified and their use in schools challenged. Historical inaccuracies running through the textbooks must also be exposed and corrected. Parents, teachers, and students would not tolerate textbooks stating that 2+2=5 or that the earth is the center of the solar system. However, some popular high-school textbooks and materials now in use contain equally blatant errors:

the United States had no interest in Vietnam other than assuring South Vietnam's self-determination;
the United States acted to counter Communist aggression in Vietnam from the north;
the North Vietnamese would not permit free elections as prescribed by the 1954 Geneva Accords;
the United States was always willing to negotiate, while the North Vietnamese were not.

On the issue of negotiations, of all of the 28 textbooks examined, only one qualified the official government statement that prior to the 1968 negotiations the United States was always willing to negotiate but the North Vietnamese refused. This single exception states, "At least one North Vietnamese offer to talk peace was turned down by the United States."[4] In addition, none of the texts, either from a moral or a tactical point of view, questioned President Johnson's use of intensive bombing to force the North Vietnamese to the bargaining table. Instead, one reports that President Johnson "hoped that North Vietnam would agree to begin peace negotiations if the United States would stop the bombing,"[5] while noting some public dissent.

Further examples of the kind of historical material omitted from the textbooks are: (1) a 1964 offer by North Vietnam to send an emissary to talk with an American emissary in Rangoon, Burma; refused by the United States;[6] (2) a North Vietnamese peace feeler delivered through France in February 1964; America bombed the North;[7] and (3) in December 1966 North Vietnam agreed to direct peace discussions; President Johnson ordered raids near Hanoi; and North Vietnam withdrew its agreement.[8]

Just as crucial as the textbooks' distortions and omissions are their failures to either mention or elaborate on facts

critical of the United States. The textbooks fail to examine
(1) the charge of United States war crimes; (2) the full
extent of human and ecological destruction in Indochina; (3)
U.S. war planners' secret motives and strategies, as revealed
in *The Pentagon Papers;*[9] (4) the strength or significance of
the antiwar movement at home, and the tactics the government took to suppress it; and (5) the unconstitutional
exercise of Executive powers in waging war.

Whereas *The Pentagon Papers* had become public property before nineteen of the textbooks had been published,
only one [10] deemed the source worthy of mention. A few of
the revised texts, however, do make brief mention of *some* of
The Pentagon Papers' revelations. Without comment, one
revised edition, in the middle of its Vietnam War discussion,
inserted these three massively indictive sentences: "These so-
called *Pentagon Papers* revealed a shocking fact. For two
decades the Presidents of the United States, acting in secret
and without consulting Congress, had waged war, either
directly or by proxy, in Indochina. And under every President—Truman, Eisenhower, Kennedy, Johnson—the situation had deteriorated."[11]

In the prologue of that same textbook, the Vietnam War is
referred to as having "hurt our image of ourselves." But we
are quickly reassured that "while there is reason for us to
admit the imperfections of our society and the mistakes of
our leaders, there is not reason for shame or gloom."[12]

An honest accounting of the Vietnam War decades could
avoid the trap of forcing a student to choose between a
dishonest "guardian of the free world" history, or a limited
"liberal" analysis that includes military facts but refuses to
consider our corporate-dominated counterrevolutionary foreign policy. An "education" based either on the conserva-
tive-patriotic history of the war or on the so-called liberal
view—always stopping short of a critical examination of
those political and economic realities guaranteeing "Viet-
nams"—will serve to perpetuate the alienation of the young
while reinforcing the cynicism of their elders.

During the Vietnam War many developed an awareness, particularly after *The Pentagon Papers* were published, of how the process of news management and government deception worked. This lesson should serve us well in recognizing "history" in textbooks as old news management. For years many Americans have argued that we must learn from the Vietnam experience, and an obvious starting place is in the schools. Parents and teachers do have the power to insist on a history that will not commit us to repeat the government's crimes of the past. And so this book is directed to all Americans who at some time in their schooling became miseducated by dishonest textbooks and do not want more of the same visited on their children. We realize that textbooks are not the whole of one's schooling, but they do have an effect: They make it simpler for the selling of an undemocratic social order by distorting and misrepresenting the past. This book's purpose is to help us recognize the distorted textbook history of one tragic period.

NOTES

1. Henry Steele Commager, "On the Way to 1984," *The Saturday Review of Literature* 50 (April 15, 1967): 68.

2. Ibid.

3. Ibid.

4. Florence Epstein and Ira Peck, *Yesterday, Today, Tomorrow*, Vol. 4 (New York: Scholastic Book Services, 1970), p. 101.

5. Leonard C. Wood, Ralph H. Gabriel, and Edward L. Biller, *America: Its People and Values* (New York: Harcourt Brace Jovanovich, 1975), p. 769.

6. Eric Sevareid, *Look*, November 30, 1965.

7. Philippe Devillers, *University of Paris*, December 5, 1966.

8. Robert Estabrook, Washington *Post*, February 4, 1967.

9. Robert McNamara, Secretary of Defense, in 1967 commissioned a massive top-secret history of the United States' role in Indochina to cover the period from World War II to May 1968. The study, known as *The Pentagon Papers*, was motivated by a rising frustration with the Indochina War among McNamara and his Pentagon colleagues. Written by thirty-six anonymous government historians (mostly State and Defense department academicians), and although far from a complete history, *The Pentagon Papers* constitute a huge archive of government decision making on

Indochina for three decades. While the analysts agree in general that the United States involvement in Indochina was a costly mistake, they uncritically accept their government's official ideology. Hence one *Pentagon Papers* historian asks whether the United States *can* "overcome the apparent fact that the Viet Cong have 'captured' the Vietnamese nationalist movement while the GVN (Saigon regime) has become the refuge of Vietnamese who were allied with the French in the battle against the independence of their nation." The historian's uncritical acceptance of an ideology committed to the use of force to guarantee the interests of United States global management prevents him from asking whether the United States *should* overcome this fact.

The United States government was unsuccessful in its attempt to block publication of the Pentagon papers because the U.S. Supreme Court ruled that their public dissemination was protected under the First Amendment to the Constitution.

10. Harry W. Bragdon and Samuel P. McCutchen, *History of a Free People* (New York: Macmillan, 1978).

11. Ibid., p. 756.

12. Ibid., xiii.

TEXTBOOK SYNTHESIS

part one

A LIST OF THE TEXTBOOKS

1. Anderson, Vivienne, and Laura Shufelt, *Your America* (Englewood Cliffs, N.J.: Prentice-Hall, 1964).

2. Bailey, Thomas, *The American Spirit*, vol. II, (Lexington, Mass.: D. C. Heath, 1978).

3. Baldwin, Leland D., and Mary Warring, *History of Our Republic* (New York: D. Van Nostrand, 1965).

4. Borden, Morton, and Otis L. Graham, Jr., *The American Profile* (Lexington, Mass.: D. C. Heath, 1978).

5. Borden, Morton, and Otis L. Graham, Jr., with Roderick W. Nash and Richard Oglesby, *Portrait of a Nation: A History of the United States* (Lexington, Mass.: D. C. Heath, 1973).

6. Bragdon, Henry W., and Samuel P. McCutchen, *History of a Free People* (New York: Macmillan, 1978).

7. Bronz, Stephen H., Glenn W. Moon, and Don C. Cline, *The Challenge of America* (New York: Holt, Rinehart and Winston, 1968).

8. Current, Richard N., Alexander DeConde, and Harris L. Dante, *United States History: Search for Freedom* (Glenview, Ill.: Scott, Foresman, 1977).

9. Eibling, Harold H., Carlton Jackson, and Vito Perrone, *Challenge and Change United States History: The Second Century*, vol. 2 (River Forest, Ill.: Laidlaw Brothers, 1973).

10. Eibling, Harold H., Fred M. King, and James Harlow, *History of Our United States* (River Forest, Ill.: Laidlaw Brothers, 1964).

11. Epstein, Florence, and Ira Peck, *Yesterday, Today, Tomorrow*, 1939–1970, vol. 4, (New York: Scholastic Book Services, 1970).

12. Frost, James A., Ralph Adams Brown, David M. Ellis, and William B. Fink, *A History of the United States: The Evolution of a Free People* (Chicago: Follett, 1968).

13. Garraty, John A., *A Short History of the American Nation* (New York: Harper and Row, 1974).

14. Graff, Henry F. and John A. Krout, *The Adventure of the American People: A History of the United States* (Chicago: Rand McNally, 1973).

15. Graff, Henry F., *The Free and the Brave* (Chicago: Rand McNally, 1977).

16. Harlow, Ralph Volney, and Hermon M. Noyes, *Story of America* (New York: Holt, Rhinehart and Winston, 1961).

17. Hofstadter, Richard, William Miller, and Daniel Aaron, *The United States: The History of a Republic* (Englewood Cliffs, N.J.: Prentice Hall, 1967).

18. Kolevzon, Edward R., *The Afro-Asian World: A Cultural Understanding* (Boston: Allyn Bacon, 1972).

19. Lippe, Paul, *The World in Our Day* (New York: Oxford Book Company, 1972).

20. Muzzey, David S., and Arthur S. Link, *Our American Republic* (New York: Ginn and Co., 1963).

21. Ralston, Leonard F., and Harold Negley, *A Search for Freedom: Basic American History* (Philadelphia: J. P. Lippincott, 1973).

22. Reich, Jerome R., Arvarh E. Strickland, and Edward R. Biller, *Building the United States* (New York: Harcourt Brace and Jovanovitch, 1971).

23. Schwartz, Sidney, and John R. O'Connor, *The Age of Greatness— Since the Civil War: Exploring Our Nation's History* (New York: Globe Books, 1975).

24. Todd, Lewis Paul, and Merle Curti, *Rise of the American Nation* (New York: Harcourt Brace Jovanovich, 1977).

25. Weinstein, Allen, and R. Jackson Wilson, *An American History: Freedom and Crisis, Since 1860*, vol. 2 (New York: Random House, 1974).

26. Wickens, James F., *Highlights of American History: Glimpses of the Past*, vol. 2 (Chicago: Rand McNally, 1973).

27. Wilder, Howard, Robert P. Ludlum, and Harriett McCune Anderson, *This is America's Story* (Boston: Houghton Mifflin, 1978).

28. Wood, Leonard C., Ralph H. Gabriel, and Edward L. Biller, *America: Its People and Values* (New York: Harcourt Brace and Jovanovich, 1975).

Origins of United States Involvement in Vietnam

TEXTBOOK HISTORY

America's involvement in the Vietnam War began "in 1950" (8:592),* "in the spring of 1950" (2:962), "in the 1950's" (9:406), "in 1954" (4:333), "in the spring of 1954" (20:686), and "in 1953 and 1954" (28:767).

The origins of the Vietnam War can be traced back to the end of World War II with the efforts of France to reassert its dominance in Indochina. France had controlled the region since the late 19th century and "resentment against (their) rule was widespread" (19:154). The Vietnamese nationalist movement emerged because of this colonialism and a desire "to be free of any foreign control" (11:98). One of the leaders of the nationalist movement was Ho Chi Minh, "a Moscow-

*The numbers in parentheses refer to the number and page of the textbook quoted; thus (8:592) is Current, DeConde, and Dante, *United States History*, p. 592. See page 3 for the list of textbooks and their reference numbers.

trained . . . Communist" (19:154) who founded the Vietnamese Independence League (Viet Minh) during World
War II to fight the Japanese, who had invaded Indochina
and taken over from the French. "An intelligent and
dedicated leader" whose main concern was the expansion of
"Communist influence" (18:359), he wanted Vietnam to be
"free of colonial domination" (7:775).

Many Vietnamese engaged in guerrilla warfare against the
Japanese, led by the Viet Minh; all of these guerrilla groups
received aid from the United States. At the end of the war the
Viet Minh continued to fight for independence against the
French, who had returned "to carry on the business of
empire as usual" (25:730). By this time, however, they "had
become little more than the nationalist front for the Vietnamese communist party" (17:835).

In September 1945 the Viet Minh proclaimed the independent Democratic Republic of Vietnam (DRV), with Ho as its
president; and in March 1946 this new government was
"recognized as a 'free state' within a French union" (17:835).
However, French commanders in southern Vietnam, who
were trying to set up a separatist state, clashed with those
who were supporting the Viet Minh government. The Viet
Minh, leading "a popular revolt with the backing of the
Chinese Reds" (3:743), began "harassing the French"
(13:462), and in response France sent troops to fight the
Communists, "who had been trained and equipped from
Russia and Red China" (10:580).

By December 1946 the war between the French and the Viet
Minh had begun. "The free world shuddered, for if the
Communists won . . . [they] might gain control of all of
Southeast Asia for awhile" (10:580). However, the Vietnamese desire for "complete independence brought much
support to the rebels" (16:784), "strong support from the
peasants" (7:775), and "even the anti-French educated
groups" (18:359). While not all Vietnamese took the side of
the rebels, most of them "refused to help the French" (11:98).

When the French-Indochina War broke out, the United

States was faced with a serious dilemma: It had to choose between aiding the French and thus violating anticolonial beliefs, or aiding a nationalist movement that was also Communist. The United States "at first tried to remain neutral. It did not help the French or the Viet Minh" (8:592). This position changed in 1949 when the French "set up an 'independent' state of Vietnam . . . an anti-Communist front" (8:592), headed by the emperor Bao Dai. This was one of the various ways the French attempted to gain popular support within Vietnam for their effort against the Viet Minh.

The United States aided the French only after "it became clear that Communist China was actively aiding the Viet Minh" (24:688); thus President Truman recognized the independent State of Vietnam and "countered with economic and military assistance to the French" (13:462). In 1950 the Viet Minh regime was recognized by Communist China, and its political emphasis was now Communist rather than nationalist. The Chinese had been "stopped" (28:687) in Korea and thus had turned their attention to Vietnam. The end of that war now allowed them to "greatly [increase] their aid" (20:686) to the Viet Minh. Ho Chi Minh's forces also "received aid from the Soviet Union" (23:668).

As the conflict in Vietnam dragged on, "the French position grew weaker despite substantial United States aid, which was prompted by the fear that the loss of Indochina would lead to the loss of all Southeast Asia to Communist forces" (12:618). All of the states in the region would fall "like a row of dominoes. . . . This was known as the 'domino theory'" (8:592). Thus, in order to block the possibility of Communist expansion, both the Truman and Eisenhower administrations supported the French forces in Vietnam. "The justification offered for this policy was not that we wished to strengthen . . . colonialism . . . but rather that a military success by international Communism" (19:154-55) had to be avoided. However, both Truman and Eisenhower "erroneously denounced the . . . anticolonial movement as part of a worldwide Communist conspiracy and considered Ho merely a Chinese puppet" (26:458). "The situation became critical in 1953 and 1954" (28:767), despite U.S. support. The United States had hoped to contain the Communists by giving money and arms to the French, but the French military position continued to crumble. The war had been "handled badly by the French commanders and was a serious drain of French blood and resources. At the end it was being continued only with massive American aid" (3:743). U.S. aid to the French amounted to "two-thirds of the cost of the . . . military effort, or about $1 billion per year" (17:835) by the end of 1953, or a total of "more than three billion dollars" (16:784) for the entire war. This aid became essential because of the lack of support in France for the conflict. "The unsuccessful and costly struggle . . . became extremely unpopular with the French people. When a new Premier . . . took office in Paris in 1954, he was pledged to end the Indochina War" (19:155).

The Viet Minh continued to make gains and in 1954 "made an all-out drive" (1:651). By that time they "had all but driven the French army from North Vietnam" (25:730), an army that still had hundreds of thousands of soldiers, "most of them Vietnamese loyalists and foreign mercenaries" (2:962). The key event that ended the conflict was the battle of Dien Bien Phu, a fortress town in northern Vietnam, where the French main army of "20,000 soldiers" was "trapped" (13:463) or "allowed itself to be trapped" (17:835) by Ho and the Viet Minh forces.

The French appealed to the United States for military assistance, and Secretary of State John Foster Dulles "prepared to take the nation to the 'brink of war' by approving plans for an American air strike" (20:685) against the Communist forces that were massing at Dien Bien Phu. The plan fell through, however, because "Eisenhower refused to get into a 'hot' war without support from Congress" (6:728), and the British also refused to back it. Eisenhower and most of his advisers "were willing to intervene" (8:678) on behalf of the French, but not without domestic and allied support. Finally, in May 1954, the French army at Dien Bien Phu surrendered.

In May 1954 a nine-power conference met in Geneva "to hammer out a peaceful solution" (2:964) to the French-Indochinese conflict. The delegates were from the United States, the Soviet Union, Great Britain, France, Communist China, and the French Indochinese states. The Geneva Agreements, which were "practically dictated" (3:743) by Communist China, included a truce between the Viet Minh and the French, "the latter acting openly for the Saigon puppet regime" (17:836). Vietnam was divided temporarily at the 17th parallel, "pending mutual withdrawal of troops, the transfer of population, and the holding of free elections. The assumption was that Vietnam would then become united and Communist" (2:964). Both the United States and the Saigon regime were alarmed by the settlement and refused to sign the Agreements. One of the reasons the Viet Minh agreed to a settlement was that the Agreements promised elections to be held in 1956 to reunify the country. The Communists expected to win these elections, but they were never held; instead, Dulles "helped install a pro-American Catholic, Ngo Diem, as head of South Vietnam" (25:730).

Although the United States made it clear that it was not happy with the Agreements, Eisenhower stated that, "'in compliance with the obligations and principles . . . of the United Nations Charter'" (17:836), it would not use "'force' or the 'threat of force'" (2:964) to disturb the Agreements. "In short, we were not happy with the situation . . . but we acknowledged that we were in no position to do anything about it" (19:155). The United States was deeply concerned about further aggression, and when it did occur, "obviously with the encouragement of North Vietnam" (2:964), it did not feel obligated to uphold the declaration it had issued at the close of the Geneva conference, in which it had pledged to avoid the use or threat of force to upset the Agreements.

France soon withdrew from Vietnam, "but that did not leave the South open to the Viet Minh. The United States moved into this vacuum" (6:728) and supported Diem's shaky, anti-Communist regime. With the country's partition, therefore, there were two governments in Vietnam: The northern half had been "surrendered to Communist domination" (14:757) under Ho Chi Minh, "the leader of Vietnam's fight for independence" (15:678), while in the South, under Diem, "free Vietnamese occupied the land" (18:359). The "free nation" (22:646) of South Vietnam, afraid that the Communists "would take over" (23:668), appealed to the United States for support. The United States responded to this request because it feared that "Southeast Asia might fall to the Communists" (14:757).

TEXTBOOK CRITIQUE

The texts obviously differ as to the beginning of United States involvement in the Vietnam War. The first real U.S. interest in the French-Vietnamese struggle began in the World War II years when discussions at Cairo, Teheran, and Yalta among Chiang Kai-shek, Churchill, Roosevelt, and Stalin attempted to deal with the problems of Indochina.[1] (The first direct involvement by the United States in Vietnam, however, was in 1845, when the U.S. *Constitution* made an attempt to force the release of a French bishop.[2]) After World War II the first direct involvement by the United States in Vietnamese affairs came with the recognition of the French-supported Bao Dai regime in Saigon in February 1950. In May 1950 President Truman approved $10 million in military assistance, and the U.S. informed Bao Dai of its intent to establish an economic mission to Vietnam.[3] Thus 1950 can be seen as a key turning point in U.S. involvement, but only two texts point to that date, and most cite our entrance to the early 1950s.

The discussions in the texts of the French-Indochinese War as France attempted to regain control of Vietnam is adequate for the most part, but a number of problems remain. While the texts note that the Viet Minh were receiving aid from China and the Soviet Union, it is never mentioned that this assistance was quite small in relation to the U.S. support of the French (according to one text, a total of $3 billion during the war). If the ratio of later (1966–73) U.S./Chinese-Soviet assistance held true for this period (according to official U.S. sources, about 29:1),[4] then the total Chinese-Soviet aid to the Viet Minh amounted to about $100 million in all. Thus simply stating that China and the Soviet Union aided Ho Chi Minh's forces, without putting it into some form of comparative context, is meaningless. This also applies to the statement that China greatly increased its aid to the Viet Minh at the conclusion of the Korean War. It is mentioned that by the end of that war, the United States was supporting the French with more than $1 billion in aid per year; yet no figure is given for the Chinese support. Thus no relevant judgment can be made, between the United States and China, and between earlier and later Chinese aid.

For centuries the Vietnamese people have waged a struggle against foreign invaders that included China, France, the Japanese in World War II, and lastly the United States. They accepted aid from the Soviet Union and China in the struggle against the U.S., but it is incorrect to state that they were pawns of an international Communist conspiracy. Only one text pointedly criticizes both Presidents Truman and Eisenhower for concluding that the Vietnamese anticolonial effort was simply part of this worldwide Communist effort, and that Ho Chi Minh was merely a Chinese puppet. This is the only text that makes a critical comment—although in only one sentence—on the relation of the nationalist struggle to the larger relations between the United States, China, and the Soviet Union.

Some texts mention the colonial nature of French rule in Vietnam and comment on the popular support that Ho Chi Minh and the Viet Minh had in the struggle against the French, but the glaring contradiction of U.S. support for an admittedly oppressive rule is rarely addressed (except for the statement that we backed the French because of the fear of a military success for international Communism). The texts do not follow the logic of their own descriptive statements about French rule to the necessary conclusion: Although the Vietnamese clearly supported the Viet Minh against the French, the United States decided to back the oppressive colonial forces, using as its rationale the threat of international Communism and the "domino theory" to convince the American people that this opposition to a genuine nationalist struggle was justified. The theory stated that if one nation fell to the Communists all the other nations in the region would also be overrun, just as a stack of dominoes would collapse if the first one fell over. No analysis of the theory is presented, other than briefly stating the basic reason for U.S. involvement and support of the French. What was behind this fear on the part of U.S. officials? The texts offer no analysis of this basic question, nor do they suggest that this theory actually served as the ideological justification for French—U.S. imperialist efforts, under the guise of defending the free world against Communism.[5]

None of the texts suggests that, despite French recognition of the independence of the DRV as part of a French union of states (one text does mention this), the United States was clearly supporting an aggressive war upon "the only legal government" in Vietnam.[6] Thus subsequent efforts by French officers to set up a separatist state in southern Vietnam, give assistance to the Bao Dai regime in Saigon, and sustain continued U.S. support for the French army, fail to address the central issue. Any and all aid to these forces was clearly violating the sovereignty of the DRV government.[7] Since the DRV had been recognized as the legitimate government, reference to their supporters as *terrorists* (found in one text) is incorrect. If the term may be applied to any group, it would relate to those French officers who overthrew DRV officials in the South. It is an incredible twist of language and truth to define the supporters of the only legitimate government as terrorists and those trying to overthrow it simply as French officers.

Only one text mentions public opinion in France on the war, noting that it had become extremely unpopular. There is no explanation of this comment, however. And only one text mentions that the majority of the troops fighting the Viet Minh were not French, but Vietnamese loyalists (loyal to the Bao Dai regime) and foreign mercenaries. Once again, a background analysis of the war could have helped students judge the relative merits of the opposing sides, particularly with regard to the nature of support. However, only a narrow recitation of facts is presented. Some texts do state that the Viet Minh had support in the war, but there is no mention of the profound contradiction that the French, with U.S. support, could rely only on client troops and foreign mercenaries. An analysis of these factors could have provided some answers as to why the French position continued to weaken despite billions of dollars in U.S. aid.

Despite the texts' recognition of the French as oppressive colonialists, the collapse of their army at Dien Bien Phu and their demise as a colonial power is treated in a sympathetic manner. Although a feeling of concern for this doomed army is expressed, no text comments on the human cost of this struggle for the Vietnamese people. We are told that the French either were trapped at Dien Bien Phu or allowed themselves to be trapped there. This contradiction is not resolved. Totally ignored is the fact that the French were besieged there because it was their Navarre Plan (named for General Henri Navarre, Commander of the French Union Forces in Indochina) to establish it as a major stronghold and lure Viet Minh troops there, where they could be destroyed by the firepower of French artillery. This crucial battle would break the back of the Viet Minh armies and allow the eventual withdrawal of French troops. The United States extended $385 million in military aid for this plan, which called for the build-up of French and native forces.[8] While a few of the texts mention the projected bombing effort appealed for by the French to save their army at Dien Bien Phu, and the political debate within the Eisenhower Administration on the possible course of action to take, no mention is made of Dulles's offer to French Foreign Minister Georges Bidault for two atomic bombs to be used to save the French garrison there.[9] The entire discussion of this battle is devoid of any critical explanation as to why the French could not have won the military struggle or the battle of Dien Bien Phu even if they had greater support at home or from the United States. There is no recognition that the basic purposes for which they fought, with support from the United States, were aimed at maintaining the colonial oppression of the Vietnamese, who developed a legitimate and powerful resistance movement in opposition. The judgments made in the texts on this issue, as throughout the entire history of the war, remain at the level of means and tactics. The issue of ends and basic questions, which has been raised by critics of the Vietnam War, is avoided.[10]

The section on the Geneva Conference and the Agreements is also inadequate. A number of crucial issues are either cursorily mentioned or totally ignored. Only one text discusses the significance of the new French Premier, Pierre Mendes-France, who came to power in June 1954 with a pledge to resign if an acceptable agreement to end the war was not reached by July 20, on the outcome of the talks. This put pressure on the delegates to obtain a settlement to the conflict. Also omitted is the role of the CIA in Vietnam during the Geneva Conference, and its numerous covert activities against the Viet Minh and the French.[11] Such information would have put into perspective the official U.S. declaration at Geneva on the use or threat of force to upset the Agreements.

The texts offer little comment on the French-installed emperor Bao Dai, and no mention is made of his collaboration with the Japanese during World War II. They had allowed French and native rulers to maintain local control during their occupation of Vietnam, and Bao Dai was one of those local rulers who aided this occupation. This put him in opposition to the nationalist struggle for independence. And it is not mentioned that the installation of Ngo Dinh Diem by the United States was opposed in South Vietnam and by the French.[12] Nor is it noted that he stated both during and after the Geneva Conference that he would not abide by the Agreements, and that the United States supported this position.[13]

NOTES

1. Gary R. Hess, "Franklin Roosevelt and Indochina," *Journal of American History* 59 (September 1972): 353–68; U.S. Cong., House, *United States-Vietnam Relations 1945–1967. Study Prepared by the Department of Defense*, 12 vols. (Washington, D.C.: GPO, 1971). This is the U.S. Government edition of The *Pentagon Papers* and hereafter will be cited as *The Pentagon Papers*, USG ed.

2. Truong Buu Lam, *Patterns of Vietnamese Response to Foreign Intervention: 1858–1900*, Monograph Series No. 11, Southeast Asia Studies (New Haven: Yale University Press, 1967).

3. The Senator Gravel Edition, *The Pentagon Papers: The Defense Department History of United States Decisionmaking on Vietnam*, 5 vols. (Boston: Beacon Press, 1972), I: 40–44, 64–65. This is the Gravel Edition of *The Pentagon Papers* and hereafter will be cited as *The Pentagon Papers*, GE.

4. *Congressional Record*, June 3, 1974, p. 17391.

5. Carl Oglesby, "Vietnam Crucible: An Essay on the Meanings of the Cold War," in *Containment and Change*, Carl Oglesby and Richard Schaull (New York: Macmillan, 1967), pp. 56, 73, 112, 115.

6. Philippe Devillers, "'Supporting' the French in Indochina?," in *The Pentagon Papers: Critical Essays*, eds. Noam Chomsky and Howard Zinn, GE V, 163.

7. Devillers, p. 164.

8. Dwight D. Eisenhower, *Mandate for Change* (New York: Doubleday, 1963) p. 338; George McTurnan Kahin and John W. Lewis, *The United States in Vietnam* (New York: Dial Press, 1967), pp. 34, 35.

9. Bidault was interviewed in the Academy-Award-winning film *Hearts and Minds*, Peter Davis, director, Rainbow Pictures, 1975.

10. Noam Chomsky, "The Remaking of History," *Ramparts*, vol. 13, no. 10 (August/September 1975), pp. 30–31.

11. *The Pentagon Papers*, GE I, 574; and Wilfred Burchett, "The Receiving End," in *The Pentagon Papers*, GE V, 63.

12. *The Pentagon Papers*, GE I, 182.

13. Ibid., 244–45.

2

The Diem Years:
1954-63

TEXTBOOK HISTORY

North Vietnam would violate the 1954 Geneva Agreements in a number of ways in the next two years. One million people were forced to flee to South Vietnam to escape from the terrorism, and another half-million were "forcibly restrained" (17:837) from leaving. Some 600,000 of these refugees were "Catholics identified in the Communist mind with the hated French regime" (2:964). There is "no doubt" (17:837), however, that some of them went South to help organize support for the Communists.

North Vietnam also violated the Agreements by importing weapons from China and the Soviet Union and by leaving trained Viet Minh guerrillas in South Vietnam after the truce; many of these, however, were native to the area and remained in their own villages. South Vietnam also imported arms (from the United States), but it and the United States had not signed the document. The purpose of the Agreements was to neutralize the region, but the "Reds had violated [this] with impunity" (3:790).

After Geneva, South Vietnam remained a free nation in the hands of Bao Dai, although not until January 1955 did the French actually return control of the regime to him and his "'strongman'" (17:836) Diem. The French had agreed at Geneva to withdraw their ground forces and colonists from Vietnam and were anxious to uphold the Agreements and leave the country, so the United States immediately commenced aid to the South Vietnamese government. Because of this action, North Vietnam thought the United States was going "to replace France in exploiting the region's resources" (26:458). The United States provided this assistance because after the French left Indochina, it "was quite obvious the Reds would try and take over the rest [of the region] by subversion and guerrilla warfare" (3:774). The United States recognized "the threat of a world-wide Communist domination" (10:584) and supported any free nation that was attempting to meet these challenges. The Communists' aim was "the destruction of free institutions and self-government and the establishment of Communist dictatorships" (10:584). While North Vietnam was the only nation in Southeast Asia controlled by the Communists, it was "eager to control more, if not all, of this region" (18:372) as part of a "long-range plan" (1:651) for the area. The plan would be attempted by encouraging rebellions and "sowing seeds of discord" (1:651) in the non-Communist countries.

When "insurrection" (5:252) did threaten South Vietnam, Eisenhower agreed to send additional economic aid, arms, and military "'advisers'" (14:761) to help that nation. He made this commitment because the United States feared that if South Vietnam fell to the Communists, other Asian nations would follow "like a row of dominoes" (11:99). The assistance was promised in a letter to Diem in October 1954, in which Eisenhower stated that a program of aid could be granted that government on the condition that it undertake political, economic and land reforms. This assistance was to include "the training of government officials, teachers, and even a police force" (12:650).

"North Viet Nam's loss [at Geneva] was a serious blow" (27:785) to the United States, as it allowed the Communists to expand their influence in Indochina and threaten other free nations. Because of this diplomatic setback, Dulles called a "conference of free nations" (20:686) and set up the Southeast Asia Treaty Organization (SEATO) in September 1954 in order to prevent the rest of Asia from falling under the "Communist weight" (20:686). The treaty pledged nations "to act together if any country in the region was threatened by aggression" (23:668), although members had to consult only on the possible course of action. However, none was mandated. Some nations that refused felt they did not have to fear Communism. Despite these problems, there is "little doubt" (1:651) that SEATO had some impact in preventing additional aggression.

In 1955, when Diem formally gained power in South Vietnam, he "overthrew Bao Dai's government" (8:592), or South Vietnam "voted to replace its French-controlled president with a nationalist [Diem]" (7:775). The United States immediately recognized Diem and began to supply him with aid. The critical event during this early Diem period was the national elections that were to be held in July 1956, as proposed by the Geneva Agreements. The feeling at Geneva had been that the 1956 elections would result in a unified, Communist Vietnam, and Ho Chi Minh would "take over South Vietnam" (14:760) in the process. The elections were never held, however, and each side "blamed the other" (18:375) for breaking this key provision of the Agreements. Diem, supported by the United States, "refused to allow" (15:678) the elections to be held because he did not trust the Communists in North Vietnam "to run a free election" (11:99), which would have resulted in a "regimented communist victory" (17:836) for Ho Chi Minh. But, in reality, Diem "felt he could not win" (13:497) an election against Ho Chi Minh, and varying estimates are given of the latter's chances, all favorable. Therefore, "To preclude free elections . . . and thus prevent reunification, Eisenhower recognized the southern half of Vietnam as a separate nation" (26:458).

Diem, who came from a wealthy Catholic family, was considered to be a staunch nationalist and anti-Communist by such important American Catholics as Francis Cardinal Spellman and John F. Kennedy; he was also supported by John Foster Dulles and Richard Nixon. At first, Diem faced tremendous obstacles in his attempts to resist the Communist uprising taking place in the South, and few "dared hope" (16:784) that his government would not be "taken over" by North Vietnam. But "able and courageous . . . Diem united his people, cleaned out Communist agents, and stood firm against his dangerous Northern neighbor" (16:784).

However, Diem used harsh and repressive policies, which caused many South Vietnamese to cease supporting the regime. He "suppressed opposition and ruled like a dictator," (7:775), allowed no free press, and ill-treated the nation's largest religious majority, the Buddhists. They said that Diem, a Catholic, was treating them "badly" (11:99), and he was under fire from many quarters for this "alleged persecution" (19:156). The Buddhists organized demonstrations against Diem—some committing suicide in protest—and it seemed clear that some of the monks were Communists in disguise. Madame Ngo Dinh Nhu, the wife of Diem's brother Nhu, inflamed the conflict further by referring to the suicides as "a Buddhist 'barbeque'" (2:969). After continued protests and additional suicides, Kennedy withdrew support of the regime.

While most felt that Diem was honest in his own right, the Ngo family and the regime was shot through with corruption. United States aid had to go through the government, and a large part of it was enriching South Vietnamese leaders, although some aid did go to train local officials. Despite its almost complete reliance upon U.S. aid, the Ngo family was "openly contemptuous of American policies and ideals" (3:775). Both Eisenhower and Kennedy pressed Diem for land reforms and other economic and political measures.

Although he accepted these reluctantly, the United States was hesitant "to cast him adrift" (17:837). American policy-makers were split as to what was the best policy to follow toward the regime. The opinions ranged from more military aid to a liberalization of Diem's policies. This liberalization sought for included allowing a free press and political opposition, and limiting his authoritarian control. However, despite resistance to a liberalization of his policies, and despite his regime's being "inefficient, dictatorial and unpopular . . . American economic and military support enabled him to survive" (6:732).

Diem's policies helped fuel the rebellion against the regime by the Viet Cong, the fighting arm of the National Liberation Front (NLF). The NLF was a "'shadow' government" that had been organized in the South and recognized by Ho Chi Minh in March 1960, "for the purpose of overthrowing the South Vietnamese government and seizing control of the country" (24:700) and "the 'liberation' of South Vietnam from United States 'imperialism'" (8:639). It collected taxes, "'enlisted' men and women for its fighting forces, and organized terrorism" (24:700).

The Viet Cong "Red revolutionists" (3:790), who were commanded by the North Vietnamese and Communist Chinese, began operations to take over South Vietnam in 1954 shortly after "the creation of North and South Vietnam, when [they] began raiding the countryside" (21:586); soon after the Geneva Agreements, when they "began guerrilla and terrorist activity" (25:781); when "the national elections . . . were not held [and] anti-Diem guerrillas . . . began terrorist activities" (8:592–93); in 1956, when the elections "to unite the country were not held" (25:781); in 1957, when "they began sending small bands of trained soldiers into the South" (15:678); in the late 1950s, when they "stepped up guerrilla warfare" (8:639); in 1958, when they "started to fight to take over South Vietnam" (22:646); and, in the early 1960s, "when [they] started a revolt to overthrow [the Diem] government" (23:678).

The Viet Cong, supported from the beginning by North Vietnam, the Soviet Union, and Communist China, was joined by many peasants who did not support Diem because of his authoritarian policies. Both the guerrillas and the leaders had been trained in North Vietnam, although "it is believed that at first the manpower came principally from the South" (19:155). The North Vietnamese obviously encouraged Viet Cong aggression in violation of the Agreements, turning to violence for reunification because they had given up hope of having free elections. After 1960 they gave "increasing amounts of aid to the guerrillas" (21:586).

By 1960 the Viet Cong had been successful. It had gained the support of many peasants because of its promises of land, and it came to control large parts of the country. Much of this support, however, was built upon "terror," by using tactics such as ambushing "small groups of enemy soldiers [and] plant[ing] deadly booby traps in the jungles" (7:776), assassinations of local officials, and "kidnapping, torture, decapitation and wholesale murder" (2:967).

The Diem regime became increasingly "oppressive and lost the support of its citizens" (21:586); it became "increasingly shaky" (19:156), and by 1960 it was evident that it would "fall to the Communists" (28:768) unless the United States stepped in with more military assistance. In the spring of 1961 Diem appealed to Kennedy for more aid and arms. Kennedy responded, indicating that he was aware that North Vietnam had "violated the Geneva Agreements by renewing aggression" (2:969), and he promised to support the South Vietnamese in their fight for independence. He felt that if South Vietnam fell to the Communists, the rest of Southeast Asia might follow, and "he was determined to prevent this" (28:768).

As a senator in 1954, Kennedy had spoken out on the French-Indochinese War, stating that " 'no amount of American military assistance . . . can conquer an enemy . . . which has the sympathy and covert support of the people' " (6:747). When he became President, however, his view changed and he sent more military aid and advisers to study the situation. One such adviser was Vice-President Lyndon Johnson, who visited South Vietnam in May 1961. After he returned, because of an increased "threat of aggression from North Vietnam" (9:406), the United States "began a major buildup of troops" (14:761) and accelerated the program of aid. Kennedy "also sent in thousands of . . . military advisers and pilots" (23:678) to aid the regime; "many . . . were actually fighting the Vietcong" (7:776). Despite this assistance, they "continued to win the war" (23:679). When Kennedy was assassinated in November 1963, "16 thousand American troops were in South Vietnam" (22:695). These troops "were serving as advisers and technicians, not as combat soldiers" (28:768), although "120 Americans had . . . been killed" (13:497) by that time.

By late 1963 the "intensity of the struggle" (18:375) in South Vietnam began to increase, and it was apparent that "no amount of money, arms, or advice would enable Saigon to hold out" (25:782) against the NLF. The war was going badly for the Diem regime, because many people in South Vietnam simply "refused to support their own government" (22:695). The Diem regime was overthrown on November 1, 1963, during a military coup led by General Duong Van Minh. The groundwork had been set for the coup when Kennedy had withdrawn his support from Diem after the Buddhist uprisings. This withdrawal of American support allowed "the militarists [to take] command, and they [murdered] their dictator" (26:458).

The United States obviously had become disenchanted with Diem, and the coup was "probably with American encouragement" (17:855), although "Lodge, the American ambassador, and American military leaders had advance knowledge of the plot" (6:748). Diem and his brother Nhu were executed by the military junta, and "[more] than ever, the United States was running South Vietnam" (6:748).

TEXTBOOK CRITIQUE

Some of the texts note that South Vietnam remained a free nation after the signing of the Geneva Agreements, with Emperor Bao Dai and Premier Diem in control, but, in fact, South Vietnam was a creation of the United States. This was in violation of the Agreements, which had set up two zones, not two countries.[1] Without the U.S. aid and arms, Diem could not have consolidated his power in this early period and ousted Bao Dai. The texts state either that he overthrew Bao Dai or gained power in 1955 because he, Diem, was considered to be a nationalist. He was not tainted by collaboration as was Bao Dai; for although Diem had worked for the French in the 1930s, he had resigned and eventually went into exile. This made him appear to be a nationalist, particularly when compared to the discredited emperor, who had actively supported both the French and the Japanese. There is no analysis of how, with U.S. support, he smashed his early political opposition, nor is it mentioned that his election victory over Bao Dai was accomplished through fraud.[2] And no mention is made of the revolutionary committee that was set up to promote Diem and conduct the election, then forced into exile after his takeover.

The texts for the most part accept the standard foreign-policy mythology about saving South Vietnam, blocking Communist aggression, and keeping it part of the free world (elements that evolved eventually into the "domino theory"). But they avoid stating the basic issue, which was who would control the destiny of Vietnam—the Vietnamese and Ho Chi Minh or the United States through Diem. It is not mentioned that the independence movement, led by men such as Ho, one of the founding fathers of Vietnam, claimed the loyalty of most Vietnamese, few of whom would consider giving their support to an aristocratic mandarin such as Diem, who had spent part of the independence struggle in exile. The war against the Diem regime crystallized around this fundamental conflict and over the larger social purposes of the regime and the Viet Minh. These purposes reflected, on one hand, the maintenance of a puppet government ultimately controlled by foreign colonialists, and on the other, the fight for national independence and socialism led by the Viet Minh. This basic conflict is almost entirely neglected in the texts.

The texts are informative concerning the numerous North Vietnamese violations of the Agreements and their terrorism toward refugees, but little is said of South Vietnamese and American violations, which began from the moment the Agreements were formalized. It is admitted that the South Vietnamese did violate the Agreements because they "abused"* (2:963) former Viet Minh guerrillas, but the reader is reminded that both South Vietnam and the United States did not sign the Agreements. The texts should have acknowledged the fact that because of U.S. refusal to sign the Final Declaration, *no* nation actually signed it. The Geneva Agreements were in two parts, the military armistice which was signed between the French and the Viet Minh, and the Final Declaration. The Declaration was supported verbally by all the national representatives except the U.S. and the Bao Dai regime. It was not signed because Secretary of State Dulles had refused to sign it for the U.S.

Students are not informed about the flow of American "advisers" (including CIA agents) into Saigon,[3] which commenced immediately after the Agreements were announced in July 1954. Nothing is said about the discipline maintained by former Viet Minh guerrillas in the South, who did not want to jeopardize the scheduled 1956 elections and therefore avoided conflicts with the Diem regime.[4] The large-scale suppression of these former resistance fighters as Diem moved swiftly against them and their peasant and urban support is ignored by the texts. This campaign included executions, extensive military expeditions and

---

*In these texts North Vietnam almost always terrorizes, never merely abuses; whereas South Vietnam abuses and represses but never stoops to terrorization.

manhunts, torture, and forced imprisonment in political "reeducation" concentration camps, some of which were assisted by members of the Michigan State University—CIA project. The Michigan State University Group trained and provided guns and ammunition for Diem's police, civil militia and "South Vietnam's version of the FBI."[5] It also served as a front for the CIA in the South during these years. No mention is made of the specific assassination campaign conducted by members of the Diem militia against former Viet Minh and other political opponents, which, according to official South Vietnamese information, took an estimated 22,000 lives.[6]

Following the Geneva Agreements, from 1954 to 1956, the DRV (North Vietnam) was accused by South Vietnam and the United States of continual violations. However, the unanimous finding of the International Control Commission (ICC) was that the major source of violations and obstruction came from the Diem regime. Countless cases of reprisals were reported to the ICC from South Vietnam, but it was unable to check them because the regime refused to cooperate.[7] A reader of these texts would be unaware of these facts.

The refugee issue is another example of how brief descriptions of events devoid of historical context prohibit the student from making objective judgments. It is stated that 600,000 of the refugees were "Catholics identified . . . with the hated French regime." However, it is not mentioned that some of these Catholics had organized their own militia and fought with the French as collaborators in the colonial oppression of their own people; that U.S. assistance in this refugee movement was actually led by the CIA and U.S. military intelligence, through a propaganda campaign which included threats of atomic bombs on the "pagans" who remained in the North and leaflets telling Catholics that the Virgin Mary had gone to South Vietnam.[8] The texts essentially tell a tale of people escaping the terrors of Communism, with little attempt to put that escape into an accurate perspective.

The texts are fairly adequate in describing the range of views surrounding the promised 1956 elections, from Diem's distrust of the Communists to his fear that Ho Chi Minh would win the election. No mention is made of the fact that at least six times from 1956 until as late as 1960,[9] the DRV asked Diem to consult about holding elections and that Diem refused because it would appear he had supported the Agreements. The *Pentagon* historians suggest that the United States did not "connive" with Diem in blocking the elections, but neither do they state the truth—that the United States did not force this provision of the Agreements upon the Diem regime, because it would have resulted in a victory for the Vietnamese and Ho and a staggering defeat for the United States and an end to our involvement there.[10] The profound influence of the election's cancellation—a crucial event in the history of the Diem era and an influence on everything that followed in the next seven years—is not examined in the texts.

The texts' description of the Diem regime's suppression and corruption is sufficiently accurate in and of itself, but no effort is made to connect this suppression (which the United States was both aware of and complicit with)[11] with the political situation. For example, it is stated that Diem mistreated the Buddhists, who had organized demonstrations and were being used by the Communists for subversive purposes. But there is little underlying analysis to permit an adequate understanding of the crisis in 1963. No mention is made of the key event that marked the beginning of the crisis: On May 8, 1963, in the city of Hué, Diem troops fired upon a crowd celebrating Buddha's birthday; nine people were killed. And nothing is said about the justification for this act (later determined to have been fabricated), that the incident began when a Viet Cong agent threw a grenade into the crowd. There is little appreciation of the depth to which this crisis mobilized sentiment against Diem, and no mention is made of the subsequent military attacks in August upon Buddhist pagodas throughout South Vietnam, which further alienated Diem from the people.

While the texts do provide students with some accurate descriptive comments on the nature of Diem's rule in South Vietnam, there is little commentary on the specific nature of this general oppression. Students learn nothing from the texts about the Diem regime's pacification program in rural South Vietnam; the stated purpose was to secure the peasants from NLF terrorism, but it actually served to create a network of quasi-concentration camps in the countryside that were used by the regime to suppress peasant support for the NLF. This program was acclaimed by U.S. officials right up to its collapse with the end of the regime itself in November 1963.

The texts' description of the origins of the revolutionary struggle against the Diem regime and of the role of the NLF range from the "outside agitator" thesis to the position that conditions under the regime provoked struggle. More importantly, there is little discussion of the objective social conditions within South Vietnam that may have brought this about. Also, the emphatic criticism of the NLF, particularly regarding the terroristic nature of its growth, precludes, for example, an analysis of the use of terrorism as a selective weapon of guerrilla warfare; in fact, it was often welcomed by peasants when directed against corrupt, brutal, or merely despised officials. Students are given the balanced view that both sides used harsh methods upon the peasantry, which, again, effectively closes discussion of why one side (the NLF) consistently grew and won support, while the other side (the Diem regime) consistently declined in influence.

Information about the downfall of the regime, about the differences among U.S. policy-makers toward Diem, and about U.S. disenchantment with him is minimal and inadequate. It minimizes U.S. involvement in his downfall, and there is little indication (except for one text that comments that the coup probably had American support, and another which accurately indicates that American Ambassador Lodge and U.S. military leaders knew about the plans) that American officials were deeply involved in the efforts to remove Diem and worked closely with the generals

who overthrew him and his brother Nhu.[13] Students given
little understanding of Diem's client role will not comprehend why it was necessary to get rid of him when he had
become a political liability. Nothing is said of U.S. planning
for the period immediately after the coup, during which it
stipulated that the South Vietnamese generals were not to
show up at the U.S. Embassy lest it appear they were signing
in for approval.[14]

The massive American aid given to the Diem regime could
not keep it afloat, and near the end of his regime, no amount
of aid, arms, and advice could save Saigon. Once again the
glaring contradiction of trying to save such a regime goes
unnoticed, and the fundamental issue of basic ends and
purposes is avoided (except on those occasions when the
texts clearly condemn the NLF or Viet Cong for their
terroristic activities; and no such analysis, of course, applies
to American actions). The question remains: Should the
Diem regime have survived? Should a regime clearly identified by our texts as oppressive have claimed billions in aid
and weapons and the moral support of the United States?
Not only is this question never answered, but it is not even
asked.

NOTES

1. The Geneva Agreements on the Cessation of Hostilities in Viet Nam, July 20,
1954, Chapter 1, Article 1.

2. Bernard Fall, *The Two Viet-Nams* (New York: Praeger, 1963), p. 257.

3. Nina Adams, "The Last Line of Defense," in The Senator Gravel Edition, *The
Pentagon Papers: The Defense Department History of United States Decisionmaking on Vietnam*, 5 vols. (Boston: Beacon Press, 1972): 5:152. This edition
hereafter will be cited as *The Pentagon Papers*, GE.

4. Joseph Kraft, Introduction to Jean Lacouture, *Vietnam: Between Two Truces*
(New York: Random House, 1966), p. xii.

5. Wilfred Burchett, "The Receiving End," in *The Pentagon Papers: Critical
Essays*, eds. Noam Chomsky and Howard Zinn, GE V, 66; Joseph Buttinger,
Vietnam: A Dragon Embattled, 2 vols. (New York: Praeger, 1967), p. 976;
Noam Chomsky and Edward S. Herman, *Counter-Revolutionary Violence:
Bloodbaths in Fact and Propaganda* (Andover, Mass.: Warner Modular

Publications, 1973), p. 17; Warren Hinkle, Robert Scheer and Sol Stern, "The University on the Make," *Ramparts Vietnam Primer* (San Francisco: Ramparts Press, 1966), p. 54; Jeffrey Race, *War Comes to Long An* (Berkeley: University of California Press, 1972), pp. 37, 40.

6. Charles Haynie and John Heckman, *The Rebellion Against the Diem Regime, 1957–58* (Ithaca, N.Y.: Cornell Ad-Hoc Committee to End the War in Vietnam, 1965), p. 14.

7. Marvin Gettleman, ed., *Vietnam: History, Documents, and Opinions on a World Crisis* (Greenwich, Conn.: Fawcett, 1965), p. 164.

8. Noam Chomsky, "The Pentagon Papers as Propaganda and History," in *The Pentagon Papers: Critical Essays*, eds. Noam Chomsky and Howard Zinn, GE V, 188; Robert Scheer, "Hang Down Your Head Tom Dooley," *Ramparts Vietnam Primer* (San Francisco: Ramparts Press, 1966), pp. 14–21.

9. Haynie and Heckman, p. 8.

10. Noam Chomsky, *For Reasons of State* (New York: Random House, 1973), p. 104; Philippe Devillers, "'Supporting' the French in Indochina?," in *The Pentagon Papers*, GE V, 177; Edward S. Herman and Richard DuBoff, *How to Coo Like a Dove While Fighting to Win: The Public Relations of the Johnson Policy in Vietnam*, 2nd ed., rev. (New York: Clergy and Laymen Concerned About Vietnam, 1969), pp. 5–6; George McTurnan Kahin, Address to the InterFaith Seminar for Clergy on Vietnam, Boston University, October 1, 1965, pp. 3–4.

11. Haynie and Heckman, p. 11; David Hotham, "General Considerations of American Programs," in *Vietnam: The First Five Years*, ed. Richard Lindholm (East Lansing: Michigan State University Press, 1959), p. 347; *The Pentagon Papers*, GE I, 252.

12. *The Pentagon Papers*, GE II, 207, 239, 250–51, 259.

13. Ibid., 269–70.

3

Escalation—"Vietnamization"— End of the War

Escalation Under President Johnson

In August 1964 North Vietnamese torpedo boats attacked U.S. destroyers in the Gulf of Tonkin. "In spite of some uncertainty about what had happened, the President announced on August 4, 1964, that two American destroyers had been attacked in the Gulf of Tonkin by North Vietnamese patrol torpedo boats and that he had immediately ordered retaliatory attacks" (24:699). President Johnson asked Congress for a resolution that would grant the Executive power to "take all necessary measures to repel any armed attack against the forces of the U.S. and to prevent further aggression" (21:588). (Later, the Gulf of Tonkin Resolution would become the subject of much debate.) Whether or not the attack was real (there was conflicting evidence), the

President now had congressional authorization to use U.S. armed forces in Southeast Asia.

The Communist-led rebels, or Viet Cong, supported by North Vietnam, were fighting "to take over South Viet Nam in 1958" (22:646). In 1964 "large numbers of soldiers from North Viet Nam invaded South Viet Nam. These Communist troops from North Viet Nam began to help the Vietcong's fight to take over South Viet Nam" (22:700-1). The United States, according to President Johnson, was engaged in the fighting "to free the South Vietnamese people from Communist aggression and to prevent the spread of communism to other countries" (11:101).

The two sides relied on different military means. North Vietnam and the Viet Cong avoided direct confrontation, using guerrilla tactics and "terrorism—bombs planted in a country marketplace or in a busy city and the torture or assassination of unfriendly village leaders" (24:700). In contrast, the Americans relied heavily on massive fire power and bombing and "search-and-destroy" operations, whereby villages that could not be held or defended by the U.S. and South Vietnam forces were burned and the people moved to refugee centers.

In February 1965, as a result of a Viet Cong surprise attack on U.S. army camps, which killed eight Americans and wounded about 125, the United States and South Vietnam retaliated by "systematic bombing of military targets and infiltration routes in North Vietnam in an effort to halt the flow of weapons and men that poured into South Vietnam" (12:649). On February 28, 1965, using the emergency powers granted by the Congress, President Johnson ordered the U.S. Air Force to bomb selected targets in North Vietnam. At first only railroads, roads, bridges, and vehicles were hit to stop the troop and supply infiltration to the South Vietnamese Viet Cong; but when this proved unsuccessful, Johnson intensified and extended the bombing to power stations and fuel dumps. "Although only military targets were attacked and the large population centers of Hanoi and Haiphong were spared, some North Vietnamese civilians were killed in bombing raids." U.S. officials "tried to limit the bombing to military targets. But many civilians were killed and many homes were destroyed" (11:100).

"In the spring of 1965, several regular North Vietnamese army units were found fighting with the Viet Cong in South Vietnam. President Johnson said that these North Vietnamese were armed aggressors from another country. Thus, he announced a new policy: the United States would be justified in sending troops to fight the aggressors openly" (7:776). This aggression by the Communists "came stealthly by infiltration routes through neutral countries or dense jungles which were difficult to police" (12:650). Johnson "hoped that North Vietnam would agree to begin peace negotiations if the United States would stop the bombing" (28:769). As the military situation worsened, Johnson "was faced with three disagreeable choices: (1) Admit defeat and pull out. . . . (2) Continue support of South Vietnamese regimes in their struggle with the Communist Viet Cong. . . . (3) Actively enter the war and attack North Vietnam" (6:756–57).

By early 1965 it had become clear to the President and his advisers that the South Vietnamese army was close to defeat, despite a numerical advantage over the Viet Cong of six to one. If the United States did not aid the South Vietnamese government, Johnson feared that "the Viet Cong, aided by North Vietnamese forces, would take over South Vietnam" (28:768). In reaction to the worsening military situation in South Vietnam, he committed American troops to battle in March 1965, and in May units of the U.S. Army and Marines began landing in increasing numbers.

President Johnson made repeated offers to negotiate with the North Vietnamese leaders and stated that he was "willing to open 'unconditional discussion'" (8:640) at any time with any of the Communist nations—the Soviet Union, China, and/or North Vietnam. Ho Chi Minh and other Communist leaders rejected his offers, calling them attempts "to fool world opinion" (11:101). The North Vietnamese refused to enter negotiations until the United States stopped the bombing and removed its troops from South Vietnam. Conversely, the United States declared it would end hostilities when the Communists withdrew their aid to the Viet Cong. "At least one North Vietnamese offer to talk peace was turned down by the U.S." (11:101).

Substituting persuasion for force, President Johnson, in April 1965, offered $1 billion in economic aid to Southeast Asia (including North Vietnam) as soon as the fighting ended. Then in May the President halted the bombing. But "the National Liberation Front and the North Vietnam government refused to end the fighting" (22:701). The U.S. resumed bombing and committed more troops to fight the Viet Cong. Again, in December 1965, the "United States tried to make peace, but once again failed," (22:701) and "despite temporary halts in the bombing of North Vietnam and appeals to the government of North Vietnam, the war went on" (27:708). President Johnson was determined "to accept no end of the war that would surrender South Vietnam to the Communists" (28:770).

South Vietnam, unstable politically, moved through a succession of military governments and was beset by deep religious and political divisions: "Buddhist groups opposed Roman Catholics and each other, while the war against the Viet Cong sometimes played a secondary role" (12:651). Air Marshal Nguyen Cao Ky took control of the government in June 1965 and began to restore some order to the country. In September 1966 he called for elections for a two-house National Assembly, and in the autumn of 1967 Nguyen Van Thieu became President and Ky, Vice-President. The elections were orderly despite the Viet Cong's attempts to try "everything including violence to sabotage the elections" (24:701). About 51 percent of the eligible voters cast ballots.

The validity of the election as a democratic procedure was widely questioned in view of the fact that the successful candidates controlled the balloting machinery, as well as the army, the police, and all media of mass communications . . . and even so won no more than about 35% of the votes cast. There were charges of fraud, corruption, and terrorism. The leading civilian candidate in the race for the presidency, who had run a fairly close second to Thieu, was promptly jailed on charges of being "pro-Communist" and still remained in custody years later. On the other hand, it was pointed out that 80% of the eligible voters took part in the election, and that foreign observers found the balloting procedures generally fair. The South Vietnamese people, it was emphasized, *had* been given a choice—which was a great deal more than could be said for North Vietnam. (19:156)

As U.S. participation in the war increased, so did criticism of its policy in Vietnam. Critics of U.S. policy argued that "the United States had no business being in Vietnam" (14:761), and some saw the struggle as basically a civil war, whereas supporters of the policy argued that "the government was not doing all it could to win" (15:679). Thus the war became a debate between hawks (supporters) and doves (critics). The doves felt that distant Vietnam was not vital to U.S. national security, that the United States had gone far beyond its pledge to help South Vietnam, and that hundreds of thousands of troops and billions of dollars were accomplishing only a military stalemate. Some feared that an escalation of the war might start a third world war, while others maintained that the U.S. was not defending freedom and democracy in South Vietnam—as the hawks claimed— because the government did not have "the support of many of its own people" (28:768) and "the military leaders are in charge of running the government" (18:370).

President Johnson was accused of using force instead of diplomacy by his escalation of the numbers of ground troops and the increased bombing. Supporters of the Administration's policy argued that bombing pauses did not result in North Vietnam's willingness to negotiate, but instead allowed it time to infiltrate more men and arms to South Vietnam's Viet Cong. The critics of escalation argued that the United States was seeking a military solution to a political problem and questioned the Administration's belief that the Communist countries (particularly Communist China) would stand aside as the escalation increased. On moral grounds the critics "objected to the massive aerial bombings (more explosives were dropped on Vietnam between 1964 and 1968 than on Germany and Japan combined in World War II), to the use of napalm and of other chemical weapons such as the defoliants that were sprayed on forests and crops, wreaking havoc among noncombatants, and to the direct killing of civilians by American troops" (13:498–99).

The dissent ranged from an extreme dove position, calling for complete withdrawal from Vietnam as soon as possible, to the hawk position, calling for a military victory to stop the spread of Communism in Southeast Asia. "Until early in 1968 public opinion polls revealed that the hawks represent the dominant opinion among the American people . . . instinctively support[ing] their country in war and trust-[ing] the President of the United States" (6:760). Those who took the middle position between these two extremes felt that the war had been "a grave mistake"; they rejected the Administration's analysis that "the principal enemy was the Communist government of North Vietnam" (24:702) and maintained that the U.S. policy "was destroying South Vietnam in the process of 'saving it' from Communists" (24:702). All critics used the rising costs in terms of casualties and money to urge adoption of their positions—either to win, to negotiate (and include the NLF), or to withdraw completely. The cost of the war increased from $6.1 billion for fiscal 1966 to $20 billion for fiscal 1967, and this drastic increase placed inflationary pressure on the U.S. economy. By September 1968 American casualties "totaled more than 27,000 killed and 92,000 seriously wounded" (24:700).

Critics cited the excessive use of Presidential power in waging the war and a widening credibility gap, a result of "contradictory official pronouncements, especially about employing new means of killing and reaching for new targets" (17:861). While Johnson's conduct of the war was criticized by many, there were some that strongly supported his policy. A Gallup opinion poll taken in late 1967 showed that only 38 percent of the American people were satisfied with President Johnson's handling of his office.

The military action in the war presented a contrast in strategies between American troops and the enemy. The U.S. forces, inexperienced in guerrilla warfare, found the war difficult because the enemy was hard to identify, posing as "innocent villagers by day and [becoming] guerrilla fighters by night" (12:649). The Americans countered these methods with sophisticated technology, increased fire power, and helicopters. Assuming the offensive, the United States continued to escalate the number of U.S. troops "to beat back the threat of Communist North Vietnam, a country being supplied with arms and equipment, supplies, and advice by both the Soviet Union and Communist China" (18:375).

The war had now become largely an American war, even though 500,000 South Vietnamese army regulars were also serving. The American commander in South Vietnam maintained in the fall of 1967 that the enemy was being defeated and that within two years or less the U.S. would be able to start withdrawing troops. Victory seemed impossible, yet "American military leaders were extraordinarily slow to grasp this fact" (13:499) and urged the President toward "one more escalation [that] would break the enemy's will to resist" (13:499). Johnson followed their advice and the escalation continued, but so did criticism of his policy; "by the end of 1968, over half a million United States troops were stationed there" (15:680).

In early 1968 the Viet Cong and North Vietnamese regulars launched their biggest attack of the war—the Tet offensive. It was directed toward thirty provincial capitals held by South Vietnam achieving "partial control of or terrorizing 26 provincial capitals" (24:701). The Viet Cong took control of large areas of rural territory left unprotected as the offensive "threatened every major city in South

Vietnam" (4:368), and the American and South Vietnamese forces paid a heavy price to regain a portion of the lost territory. The Tet offensive not only showed "that the 'other war'—the effort of the Saigon government to win the allegiance of the Vietnamese people—was still far from won" (24:701), but it "stunned the administration and refuted completely its optimistic statements" (26:460). The Tet offensive was a "turning point in the war" (6:761) (15:680).

In addition to the bombing pauses, President Johnson ordered a limited bombing halt in March 1968. (Two of the texts—4:368 and 5:254—confuse wars, however, and state that Johnson halted the bombing "north of the 38th parallel"—Korean War dividing line—instead of the 17th—Vietnam's dividing line). At this time he also announced that he would not seek reelection but would devote the remainder of his term seeking peace. The North Vietnamese responded positively, and in May 1968 peace talks began in Paris. However, North Vietnam, which continued to insist on unconditional American withdrawal from Vietnam, "would not even admit, in spite of undeniable evidence, that regular units of their army were engaged in South Vietnam (or Cambodia, or in Laos)" (19:162). The United States maintained that Hanoi was the government to be negotiated with, and that to allow the National Liberation Front (Viet Cong) to be seated would be to falsely assert their legitimacy. The peace talks remained stalled.

The Vietnam War became a major issue as the United States moved toward the 1968 presidential election. Johnson's escalation of the war continued to divide the nation, and the dissent particularly increased on college campuses. "Hubert Humphrey and Richard Nixon both campaigned for the presidency on a promise to end the war" (25:782). Nixon said, without specifying, that he had a plan for ending the war on "honorable" terms, and this contributed to his election victory, even though Humphrey's campaign was helped greatly by President Johnson suspending the bombing of North Vietnam shortly before the election. When Nixon took office in 1969, the Vietnam War had become America's second longest war and the third costliest in terms of lives and money expended.

Nixon's "Vietnamization" Program

President Nixon continued the American presence at the Paris Peace Conference (which now included South Vietnam and the National Liberation Front). In November 1969 Nixon announced his plan to "Vietnamize" the war through a gradual, scheduled withdrawal of American forces and a simultaneous strengthening of ARVN (Army of the Republic of Vietnam, South Vietnam) troops to take over the fighting. About 110,000 troops were to be pulled out of South Vietnam by April 1970, 25,000 in the first three months. But the war continued as the leaders of North Vietnam continued to insist on complete, unconditional withdrawal of U.S. forces.

President Nixon rejected his critics' proposals for either immediate withdrawal or for setting a deadline for the withdrawal of all troops. He maintained that the ARVN forces needed additional time for training and to be better equipped so that they were "able to defend themselves" (24:703).

"Nixon's plan was bitterly criticized on the grounds that it proposed to continue the war 'by proxy' by paying the South Vietnamese to do what we ourselves were unable to do" (19:163). The critics also pointed out that the plan would still require American involvement in Vietnam and would commit for an indefinite period some U.S. units for air support and logistics. It was believed that such a presence might be a source of provocation and lead to further hostilities. An attempt in Congress to force a deadline on our withdrawal was narrowly defeated.

One problem with the strategy of Vietnamization "was that the U.S. had been employing it without success for 15 years" (13:501). The South Vietnamese troops (ARVN) lacked "the enthusiasm for the kind of tough jungle fighting at which the North Vietnamese and the Viet Cong excelled" (13:501). Although the reasons for this were complex, the primary reason was probably "the incompetence, corruption, and reactionary character of the South Vietnamese government" (13:501).

Along with Nixon's plan for Vietnamization of the war, Secretary of Defense Melvin L. Laird in late 1969 announced a policy of "protective reaction," which would replace the "search and destroy" policy. Now the United States would engage the enemy only if attacked or if threatened with an attack. The Administration felt this plan would quiet opposition to the war by reducing American casualties. Instead, in the late 1960s large numbers of people demonstrated against the war.

Nixon's plan rested on the reaction of the North Vietnamese and the Viet Cong. If they did not de-escalate, the American withdrawal would have to be slowed or stopped. After Ho Chi Minh's death in 1969, the North Vietnamese continued to regard the United States as an illegal invader and demanded complete and unconditional U.S. withdrawal.

In December 1969 Nixon announced his intention to withdraw another 50,000 troops by April 15, 1970, and by the fall of 1970, American troop strength had been cut from the 1968 high of more than 500,000 to about 385,000. (At the end of 1971, U.S. forces had been further reduced to about 150,000 as the withdrawal program proceeded on schedule.)

In late April 1970 President Nixon startled the American public by ordering a joint U.S.—South Vietnamese invasion ("venture" [24:704]) ("incursion" [2:987]) into neutral, neighboring Cambodia, a military action that angered many who believed Nixon had been "winding down" (2:987) the war. Instead, it appeared to be escalating again, as "the United States Air Force [also] bombed North Vietnamese cities and military centers" (28:769). U.S. troops were authorized to destroy enemy sanctuaries (ammunition and arms depots and storage facilities) along the eastern border of Cambodia. Nixon promised a withdrawal within sixty days after the mission had been completed. The American public reacted with demonstrations throughout the nation, and resolutions were introduced in Congress to curb Presidential power over American military overseas. As a result of the overwhelming public condemnation of the invasion, Nixon quickly withdrew the American ground troops but intensified the air attacks.

In 1971 a U.S. Army officer was accused and convicted of "the premeditated killing of 'not fewer than 22' unarmed, unresisting Vietnamese civilians" (19:161). This "massacre" by the United States Army at My Lai in 1968 claimed the lives of "more than 100 villagers" (19:161), or "about 500 men, women and children" (8:642). This was one of many reports of American atrocities, and it led some to conclude that the United States "could be just as inhumane as the Communists" (26:460). Reports such as those from My Lai renewed the debate on why the United States was in Vietnam. Americans continued to try "to balance the war's hopeless horrors against their pride, their detestation of communism, and their unwillingness to turn their backs on their elected leader. Nixon's most bitter enemy could find no reason to think he wished the war to go on" (13:501).

An operation similar to the Cambodian invasion took place in Laos in early 1971. Although American air and artillery supported the South Vietnamese, heavy losses resulted, and opinion became even more divided as to how effective ARVN troops were without U.S. support. "Vietnamese casualties probably mounted under Nixon, as the bombing of North Vietnam and Laos was intensified" (4:381). Bases in Laos had been a staging area for military operations against South Vietnam, and evidence indicated that since the 1950s the North Vietnamese had had troops stationed in Laos. The U.S.–South Vietnamese move against these bases proved to be "an unsuccessful attempt to cut the Ho Chi Minh trails" (25:781), and the fighting continued in Laos.

In 1971 General Thieu ran unopposed for reelection as President of South Vietnam. Early in the race, Vice-President Ky dropped out, accusing Thieu of dictatorial methods and undemocratic election procedures. Thieu received an overwhelming majority of votes, with only a small number of voters dissenting by destroying their ballots. However, the elections "were hardly the showcase for democracy that the United States would have liked to see. President Nguyen Van Thieu had no one running against him, and opposition candidates for congress were unable to campaign freely. Many Americans became further disillusioned with the military effort they were making" (27:714).

While Americans at home were becoming more and more disillusioned, low morale among U.S. forces was also becoming a problem, with a relatively high desertion rate, lax discipline, and signs of widespread drug abuse and addiction. The draft system was under attack because deferments for college students meant a disproportionate number "of men from the lower socioeconomic levels and from minority groups" (19:161) were serving in Vietnam. President Nixon changed the draft system to a lottery, limited mainly to nineteen-year-olds, which meant there would be fewer deferments for married men, college students, and those in special occupations. Many considered the changes unfair, but by eliminating some of the inequities in the draft law, Nixon managed to reduce public protest against the war.

Late in March 1972 the North Vietnamese launched a number of assaults throughout South Vietnam. The President reacted with even more intensive bombing and ordered the port of Haiphong and other northern shipping ports mined in order to stop the flow of Communist supplies to North Vietnam. He also called for the bombing of Hanoi and Haiphong (neither had been bombed since 1968) and the rail lines from China, a move that was denounced by both Russia and China, although neither took any action. In May 1972 "the United States began systematic bombing of all North Vietnam and mined North Vietnamese rivers, canals, and ports—including Haiphong Harbor" (25:781). The air war replaced the ground war, and "there was no letup in the relentless fury of the air war" (24:704).

By 1972, 55,000 Americans had died in Vietnam. The war had become the fourth costliest in American history. The North Vietnamese had sustained heavy losses, but they continued their will and ability to resist. The Vietnam War appeared to be hopelessly stalemated. A major concern in the peace negotiations was the fate of American prisoners of war held by the North Vietnamese. In violation of the Geneva Agreements, North Vietnam had released only belated and fragmented information about 1,600 POW's. A peace settlement from the American point of view would have to include "the release of American prisoners of war held by the North Vietnamese and the Viet Cong" (8:644). "From the North Vietnamese side, the American prisoners in their hands provided an important factor of 'leverage' in conducting negotiations" (19:162). President Nixon knew the public was sick of the war. But if he withdrew all U.S. forces and the Saigon regime fell under Communist control, he would be blamed. He continued both the air war and the negotiations.

The final negotiations took place in the fall of 1972, and a peace-settlement draft, which included an in-place cease-fire, withdrawal of all U.S. forces from Vietnam, and return of American POW's was negotiated in October. The chief U.S. negotiator, Henry Kissinger, declared that peace was "at hand" (24:704), and this encouraging news contributed toward Nixon's reelection in November. In that 1972 election Nixon defeated Senator George McGovern, a liberal Democrat who favored complete withdrawal of the United States from Vietnam. When it was revealed that Senator Thomas Eagleton, McGovern's choice for his vice presidential running mate, had a previous mental illness problem, the indecisiveness of McGovern's response is said to have hurt his campaign.

After he was reelected President Nixon tried "to extract more favorable terms from the Vietnamese Communists." He accused the enemy of "not bargaining in good faith over the remaining details of the peace treaty" (13:503) and ordered more intensive bombing against Hanoi and other North Vietnamese cities. The bombing was also a reaction to enemy violations of the informal agreement following the suspension of bombing in 1968, and partly to take the pressure off ARVN troops and to protect U.S. forces. The United States lost many B-52 bombers in the heavy bombing raids.

In January 1973 a cease-fire peace settlement was finally reached. The North Vietnamese won control over large sections of the South, and the U.S. won release for the American POW's within 60 days. The cost of the war was high: 55,000 American troops killed, more than 300,000 wounded, and a staggering dollar cost of 140 billion. "As for the people of Southeast Asia, estimates put South Vietnamese deaths at 160,903 and those of the Vietcong and North Vietnamese at 922,295. In addition, more than 6 million refugees were uprooted and homeless. Large areas of Vietnam, Laos, and Cambodia had been devastated" (24:704).

While the war was over for the Americans, it was not over for the Vietnamese. The cease-fire "seemed almost impossible to enforce" (25:782) and "soon fell apart" (27:715), "with each side blaming the other for violations of the agreements" (24:704). Then, "early in 1975 the North Vietnamese launched a furious assault and the South Vietnamese defenses crumbled like cardboard" (2:1025). "From January to December 1975, the world watched as Indochina fell to Communist troops" (8:644). "And so, with the Communist takeover of South Vietnam, three tragic decades of fighting in Vietnam came to an end" (24:705).

TEXTBOOK CRITIQUE

The textbooks in general avoid critical inquiry and analysis. When a conflicting explanation or viewpoint on the war exists, the texts note the difference only by briefly stating the competing viewpoints. Even though well-documented evidence exists to help confirm or deny them, the texts usually ignore such evidence, allowing the students to be "objective." Thus one learns that the United States claimed Hanoi to be the aggressor government, while the North Vietnamese regarded the United States as an illegal invader. Most text criticism of the war is reduced to a brief mention of the critics' arguments: that it was basically a civil war, that the Presidential power to wage war was excessive, that there was a credibility gap.

During the war, voices critical of U.S. war policies, both in and outside the government, were drowned out by successive administrations or clouded by acquiescence on the part of the media. In effect, they were attempting to "sell" the war to the public in the early and mid-1960s. Simplistic clichés were substituted for hard analysis; the textbooks further perpetuate this public relations work. The repetition of the myths and the distortions, such as "the U.S. had limited options in Vietnam," functions to limit the analytical tools of the student because it denies any theories that at the time were regarded as subversive or unpatriotic. Repeating only this "packaged" history, the textbooks restrict the parameters of criticism and thereby inhibit the student's power of inquiry.

The texts note the dissent and criticism of the war that divided Americans: from President Johnson not keeping his campaign promise to keep the U.S. out of a land war in Asia, to U.S. support of an undemocratic regime in Saigon, to being overextended in foreign commitments. However, it is never explained that the Vietnamese were fighting for their national liberation; these words are always set off in quotation marks. Also, nowhere is it suggested that a motive for U.S. involvement could have been imperialistic, i.e., the protection of American business interests throughout the world. If U.S. imperialism is mentioned, it is also set off in quotation marks to certify that the claim is invalid. The only serious question the student is asked to contemplate is: Are we overextended in taking on all of these responsibilities in the Free World?

Only *one* of the 28 textbooks broaches the issue of "Free World versus Communist aggressors," or the "U.S. strugling for others' self-determination." This text, making no attempt at historical connections, states that the Central Intelligence Agency (CIA) "engaged in 'dirty tricks' designed to disrupt the economy of North Vietnam after the Geneva Accords of 1954," and in the next sentence states, with no explanation, that the CIA "had a hand in overthrowing governments considered unfriendly to the United States."[1]

The texts leave the student with the impression of U.S. willingness and North Vietnamese foot-dragging on the matter of negotiations. And only one text departs from this view, stating: "At least one North Vietnamese offer to talk peace was turned down by the U.S."[2] In order to understand why negotiations never seemed to work, the student would have to be aware of U.S. fear of a neutralist solution, i.e., a coalition government, which was a major stumbling block to negotiations. President Johnson in March 1964 spoke of "knocking down the idea of neutralization wherever it rears its ugly head."[3] The student should be allowed to assess the alternatives to the myth that "America pursues peace, but the enemy blocks negotiations," and to question why the United States escalated the war at every stage when negotiations seemed possible. Several studies on Vietnam recounted these actions, and in *The Politics of Escalation in Vietnam*, Franz Schurmann, et al., state: "The U.S. increased its commitment to a prolongation of the Vietnam War at a time when the drift of the Saigon junta and of public opinion was in the direction of negotiations for a neutralized Vietnam."[4]

In 1964 the North Vietnamese offered to send an emissary to talk with an American emissary in Rangoon, Burma. The United States refused the offer.[5] Early in the war, U.N. Secretary General U Thant made a number of attempts to get the warring parties together for negotiations. The American public was not informed of these peace efforts or of the rejection by the U.S. policy-makers at the time until it was reported in the New York *Times* in February 1965. But U Thant's frustration over U.S. rejection of peace proposals and the government's deception of the public goes unrelieved in the textbooks: from public conciliatory calls for negotiations, while sending secret ultimatums to Hanoi, to President Johnson treating the Tonkin Gulf incident as though it were another Pearl Harbor, keeping secret our covert programs to provoke the "enemy." *The Pentagon Papers* confirm the gap between the official versions of the war—passed along to the public by the press—and the reality of the Vietnam situation as reflected in the secret communications of the U.S. war planners. However, even before *The Pentagon Papers* revealed that history of deception, many sources moved beyond the official view and clearly demonstrated the bankruptcy of the government's version.[6] Nevertheless, the textbook authors, following in the footsteps of the uncritical press, failed to move *their* histories beyond these official views, or beyond the superficial hawk-dove clichés.

While the government was grinding out "Communist aggression" rallying arguments, the Assistant Secretary of Defense, John T. McNaughton, was admitting to his colleagues that the arguments were unconvincing to the American public. In a memo to his superior, Robert S. McNamara, McNaughton wrote:

A feeling is widely and strongly held that "the Establishment" is out of its mind. The feeling is that we are trying to impose some U.S. image on distant peoples we cannot understand (anymore than we can the younger generation here at home), and that we are carrying the thing to absurd lengths. Related to this feeling is the increased polarization that is taking place in the United States with seeds of the worst split in our people in more than a century.[7]

And further, even McNaughton's assessment of U.S. objectives differed from those rallying arguments. He listed U.S. aims by percentages of importance, stating that 70 percent of the U.S. aim would be "to avoid a humiliating US defeat" and "10% to permit the South Vietnamese to enjoy a better, freer way of life."[8]

Earlier McNaughton, in a position paper to his colleagues, reasoned that even if bombing North Vietnam did not force Hanoi to pull out the Viet Cong, it would have demonstrated that the United States was a "good doctor" and willing to "have kept promises, been tough, taken risks, gotten bloodied, and hurt the enemy very badly."[9] Of course, the war planners could not be expected to share these candid assessments with the public, any more than the planning and reasons for the war could be shared with those required to fight and die in that war.

Government by secrecy and deception is now a known fact, and it has been amply documented in the more than 7,000 pages of narrative history and documents that comprise *The Pentagon Papers*. Nevertheless, for the sake of historical accuracy alone, the *full* range of lessons of the war should be noted, even those lessons that justly criticize our policies. If American schools presented a historically accurate account of the Vietnam War, the student could begin to understand what Michael Bakunin was saying when he observed:

. . . to offend, to oppress, to despoil, to plunder, to assassinate or enslave one's fellowman is ordinarily regarded as a crime. In public life, on the other hand, from the standpoint of patriotism, when things are done for the greater glory of the State, for the preservation or the extension of its power, it is all transformed into duty and virtue.[10]

While many of the texts cite the undemocratic nature of the Saigon government, they uncritically accept the official view—discredited by *The Pentagon Papers*—that superficial reforms and morale-building programs would eventually unite the South Vietnamese around the Saigon leadership. The possibility was never considered that Vietnamese forces outside of Saigon had in fact united the people—against what they considered an alien invading army and its client regime. Instead, one text offers this: "[Saigon was] too feeble to unite their people in the struggle against the Reds."[11] And another text states as the fighting escalated in early 1965: "Although outnumbering the Viet Cong by about six to one [the South Vietnamese armies] were in danger of being defeated."[12]

An occasional noting of inevitable, unavoidable civilian casualties is accompanied in the texts by statements of the care the United States took in avoiding civilian targets during the air war. Most of the texts have accepted, on faith, the pronouncements of government and military officials while ignoring eyewitness accounts from the American and foreign press (in 1967) describing the western zone of Haiphong as a bombed-out "wasteland." These correspondents described gutted homes, food-processing plants destroyed, and whole residential neighborhoods demolished by the U.S. raids.[13] *The Pentagon Papers* reveal that the CIA had informed the Administration that American bombing had caused an estimated 29,000 civilian casualties in North Vietnam between 1965 and 1966. The texts, however, discuss civilian casualties in general terms and as being inevitable given the nature of the war. The "balanced" view is presented of both sides sharing responsibility and specific evidence linking heavy civilian casualties with massive U.S. fire-power and bombing tactics is ignored. Thus, a 1967 CIA report cited in *The Pentagon Papers* that states the magnitude of civilian casualties—80 percent of the total—is also ignored.[14]

Although some of the texts discuss other nations' violations of international law in their accounts of World War II, assessment of American violations is noticeably absent. Yet a research team studying military conduct during the war concluded: (1) "There is a legal case to be made against our actions in Vietnam and it is, we believe, a devastating one," and (2) "in instance after instance, the U.S. has far exceeded the bounds of what is morally permissible in Vietnam."[15]

Text after text describes the North Vietnamese and the Viet Cong as "terrorists" and "aggressors." The enemy seeks "domination" through "subversion." The United States "intervenes" to stop "aggression." The United States is "forced" to fight to "defend freedom." The Communists "take over"; the Americans "answer the Communists' challenge." The most frequently used word in describing the military tactics of the North Vietnamese and the Viet Cong is "terrorism." U.S. bombing, the major destructive tactic in the war[16]—7 million tons, more than twice the tonnage the United States dropped in both World War II and the Korean War—is described as "systematic," "heavy," "massive," "raining," "intensified," "retaliatory," "constant," or "stepped up"; but *never* as terror.

The Paris Peace Agreement of January 1973 and the end of the war in April 1975 are mentioned by only half of the texts published after those events transpired; and the brief statements made in those texts distort both events. No attempt is made to document which side subverted the Paris Agreement. Substituted for this historical task are: "each side blamed the other," or "the cease-fire fell apart," or "the enemy continued its aggression." No mention is made of the fact (reported in the major media at the time) that the White House rejected, and hence violated, the major principles of the Agreement when Kissinger and Nixon announced that the United States would recognize only Thieu's Saigon regime.

The end of the war in April 1975 is described, in the few texts that mention it, as a Communist takeover, but they fail to explain how a people can take over their own country. The texts never explain how an outside Communist, "terrorist" force was able to confront the most powerful and well-financed military campaign in history, defeat that power and take over Vietnam. Ignoring and suppressing historical evidence as to who actually represented the indigenous population and who aligned with the foreign forces, the texts refuse to acknowledge the victory for Vietnamese independence.

NOTES

1. Henry W. Bragdon and Samuel P. McCutchen, *History of a Free People* (New York: Macmillan, 1978), p. 786.

2. Florence Epstein and Ira Peck, *Yesterday, Today, Tomorrow* (New York: Scholastic Book Services, 1970), p. 101.

3. The Senator Gravel Edition, *The Pentagon Papers: The Defense Department History of United States Decisionmaking on Vietnam*, 5 vols. (Boston: Beacon Press, 1972) III: 511. This edition hereafter will be cited as *The Pentagon Papers*, GE.

4. Franz Schurmann, Peter Dale Scott, and Reginald Zelnik, *The Politics of Escalation in Vietnam* (New York: Fawcett World Library, 1966), p. 34. See also Harry S. Ashmore and William C. Baggs, *Mission to Hanoi* (New York: G. P. Putnam's Sons, Berkley Medallion Edition, 1968); and David Kraslow and Stuart H. Loory, *The Secret Search for Peace in Vietnam* (New York: Vintage, 1968).

5. Eric Sevareid, *Look*, November 30, 1965.

6. See numerous selections in *The Pentagon Papers*, for example, GE III, 149–52. Early covert operations under President Kennedy are cited in *The Pentagon Papers*, New York *Times* edition (New York: Bantam, 1971), pp. 90–91, 123–25, and 130–35. This edition of *The Pentagon Papers* hereafter will be cited as *The Pentagon Papers*, NYT ed.

7. *The Pentagon Papers*, NYT ed., xx.

8. *The Pentagon Papers*, GE III, 695.

9. Ibid., 582.

10. Quoted in Noam Chomsky, *For Reasons of State* (New York: Randon House, 1973), preface.

11. Leland D. Baldwin and Mary Warring, *History of Our Republic* (New York: D. Van Nostrand, 1965), p. 790.

12. Lewis Paul Todd and Merle Curti, *Rise of the American Nation* (New York: Harcourt Brace Jovanovich, 1977), p. 699.

13. See Chapter 6 and note 15 below.

14. *The Pentagon Papers*, GE IV, 136.

15. *In the Name of America*, Study commissioned by Clergy and Laymen Concerned About Vietnam (Annandale, Va.: The Turnpike Press, 1968), pp. 1-2. See also Telford Taylor (former U.S. chief counsel at Nuremberg), *Nuremberg and Vietnam:* "Somehow we failed to learn the lessons we undertook to teach at Nuremberg, and that failure is today's American tragedy." (*The Pentagon Papers*, NYT ed., p. 207).

16. The World Health Organization (WHO) of the United Nations estimated more than $1 billion destruction to Vietnam's medical facilities during the war.

A CONCISE HISTORY OF
THE VIETNAM WAR

part two

4

Origins of United States Involvement in Vietnam

"The first act of armed intervention by a Western power in Vietnam is generally held to have been perpetrated in 1845 by a ship of the United States Navy, the *Constitution*." According to Vietnamese historian Troung Buu Lam, the United States was attempting to force the release of a French bishop.[1] During the early 1800s Catholic missionaries and Western cargo and gun ships entered Vietnam in the wake of two thousands years of Chinese, Mongol, and Cambodian invasions and occupations. French colonization dates from the French army seizure of Saigon in 1859, with the complete occupation of Vietnam taking place by 1884.

French colonial rule was very authoritarian and particularly harsh on the peasants, who were forced to carry a heavy tax burden. The French also antagonized the small but influential group of Western-educated (mostly in France) Vietnamese who suffered job discrimination when they returned to Vietnam. They played an important role in the nationalist movement that emerged after World War I. This movement was also supported by Vietnamese soldiers and workers who had been sent to France to help defeat the Germans. They "came into contact with social and political ideas that were quite inconsistent with the colonial system existing at home," and some joined the struggle to overthrow French rule. In the 1920s French suppression of anti-colonial efforts drove Vietnamese nationalists underground. After 1930 the underground would be led by the Indochinese Communist Party and Ho Chi Minh, who was to be the major figure in the Vietnamese independence struggle for the next forty years. The 1930s were difficult times, however, as numerous rebellions were defeated by the French and thousands of political opponents were imprisoned.[2]

During the years of French colonization, as Vietnamese nationalist resistance increased, France assumed the role not of colonial conqueror, but of protector of the "free world," a defender against communism.

Washington aligned with this position to set the struggle in Cold War terms, which is described by George McTurnan Kahin and John W. Lewis, noted American scholars on Southeast Asia:

[In 1950] President Truman linked his decision to send American forces to Korea with the announcement of increased arms shipments to the French in Indochina and the interposition of American power between Communist and Nationalist China in the Formosa Straits. In accordance with these new American priorities, France's position of Vietnam was now described in terms of the Free World's stand against communist expansionism, and Washington ceased to perceive the war in Vietnam as primarily a local colonial conflict. Now linked to the Cold War, Vietnam was regarded as an area of strategic importance to the United States.[3]

Prior to this early 1950 Cold War stance, American policy under President Franklin D. Roosevelt was characterized by a projected public image of support for national self-determination, *but* actual commitments in support of colonialism. In the case of Indochina, the government edition of *The Pentagon Papers* describes U.S. policy toward Indochina during World War II as "ambivalent." A succession of FDR messages and high-level official statements to the French government indicate that the United States had the "intention to restore to France its overseas empire after the war." In November 1942 a letter from FDR's personal representative to General Henri Giraud assured the French leader that "it is thoroughly understood that French sovereignty will be re-established as soon as possible throughout all the territory, metropolitan or colonial, over which flew the French flag in 1939."[4] *The Pentagon Papers* conclude: "Indochina thus seemed relegated to French volition."[5]

America's emerging official position on Vietnam is reflected in a 1945 exchange of cables between Washington and its Ambassador in China, Patrick J. Hurley. On May 28, Hurley cabled Truman:

The American delegation at San Francisco seemed to support the theory of the imperial control of colonies . . . by the separate and combined imperialistic nations. . . . There is a growing opinion throughout Asia that America favors imperialism rather than democracy.[6]

In 1940 the Japanese had taken over Vietnam through an agreement with the French which gave them ultimate power while leaving local matters in French hands. In May 1941 Ho Chi Minh organized various underground nationalist groups into the Vietnamese Independence League, or Viet Minh. The Viet Minh, which led the anti-colonial struggle against the Japanese, was essentially "a nationalist-front organization, led primarily by the Indochinese Communist Party but attempting to attract Vietnamese patriots of all political hues in a common struggle against the Japanese and the French." The Viet Minh remained underground during the war, and as the leading anti-Japanese force they received American aid through the Office of Strategic

Services (OSS), the forerunner of the CIA. They helped the war effort by rescuing the American pilots and supplying information on Japanese troops. By 1945 the Viet Minh had gained control of most of northern Vietnam and were the leading opposition force. Two days after the Japanese surrendered to the Allies, Viet Minh forces took the city of Hanoi without any resistance and by September 1945 they had defeated the combined Japanese-French colonialists.[7] On September 2, 1945, President Ho Chi Minh proclaimed the independence of the Democratic Republic of Vietnam (DRV). Thus Vietnam (North and South) became the first colonial country to establish a popular democratic government after World War II.[8] Ho Chi Minh described the revolutionary nationalist struggle:

Our people have broken the chains which for a century have fettered us, and have won independence for the Fatherland. Vietnam has the right to be free and independent and in fact it is so already. The entire Vietnamese people are determined to mobilize all their physical and mental strength, to sacrifice their lives and property, in order to safeguard their freedom and independence.[9]

This independence did not last long. The Potsdam Agreement between Britain, China, the Soviet Union and the United States allowed British and Chinese troops to occupy southern and northern Vietnam respectively. They were to round up and disarm Japanese troops and release Allied war prisoners; but the British also released and rearmed 5,000 French troops who had been held by the Japanese. The troops promptly staged a coup on September 23, seizing control of Saigon from Viet Minh authorities. This coup led to military action between the Viet Minh, and British, French and Japanese troops. Additional French troops entered the conflict and by the end of 1945 they had 50,000 soldiers in southern Vietnam.[10]

There was a temporary pause in the French-Viet Minh conflict in March 1946 when France signed an agreement with Ho Chi Minh in which it "recognized the Republic of Vietnam as a Free State with its Government, its Parliament, its Treasury, its Army, within the framework of the Indo-chinese Federation and of the French Union," thus establishing the Ho Chi Minh government as "the only legal government of Vietnam."[11] However, almost immediately France withdrew its recognition of the Democratic Republic of Vietnam as a sovereignty. This came in June when the French Viceroy set up "a separate puppet government in [southern Vietnam] and recognized it as a 'free republic.'" The resulting tension finally exploded in armed conflict when the French Navy shelled Haiphong harbor on November 23, killing an estimated 6,000 civilians. The Viet Minh retaliated in December by attacking French troops in Hanoi and war soon engulfed all of Vietnam.[12] *The Pentagon Papers* shed no light on this crucial point in history but merely report that "the DRV government took to the hills to assume the status of a shadow state." "The issue of who was the aggressor has never been resolved."[13]

Philippe Devillers, director of South East Asia Studies of Centre d'Etude des Relations Internationales in Paris, reaches a more solid conclusion:

For reasons of sheer opportunism, the United States failed to tell France that it could not *ignore* the legal government of Vietnam and especially that it should not look for an alternative, through "Vietnamization" of the war. Actually, the United States agreed with this French course, and abdicated *then* all principles of morality. This *essential, fundamental* aspect of the story is totally lacking in the *Pentagon Papers*, and *therefore remains practically hidden from the American public.*[14]

In 1950 America's support for French policy in Vietnam took a more concrete form.

The dollar flow to back up the French military campaign in Vietnam grew rapidly from approximately $150 million per year in 1950 to over $1 billion in the fiscal year of 1954, when the United States was underwriting 80 percent of the cost of the war. On April 6, 1954, the U.S. announced that its aid to Indochina for the subsequent fiscal year would run to $1.33 billion. This equalled one-third of the entire American foreign-aid program and was by far its largest single component. Of this amount $800 million was "allocated through France" for "direct support" of French Union forces fighting in the Indochina theater, $300 million was for equipment to be supplied to them, and $33 million was for economic and technical assistance.[15]

The futility of that counterrevolutionary effort should have been apparent to U.S. policy-makers if they had listened to their own intelligence sources. In congressional testimony on May 11, 1972, Abbot Low Moffat, chief of the Division of Southeast Asia Affairs, Department of Defense, reflected on these past assessments:

I have never met an American, be he military, OSS [Office of Strategic Services], diplomat, or journalist, who had met Ho Chi Minh who did not reach the same belief: that Ho Chi Minh was first and foremost a Vietnamese nationalist. He was also a Communist and believed that Communism offered the best hope for the Vietnamese people. But his loyalty was to his people. When I was in Indochina it was striking how the top echelon of competent French officials held almost unanimously the same view. Actually, there was no alternative to an agreement with Ho Chi Minh or to a crushing of the nationalist groundswell which my own observations convinced me could not be done. Any other government recognized by the French would of necessity be puppets of the French and incapable of holding the loyalty of the Vietnamese people.[16]

In May 1954, despite American aid to the French efforts to crush the Vietnamese struggle for independence, France's military power suffered a decisive defeat at Dien Bien Phu. The French Indochina War was over.

In January and February 1954 the Four-Power Foreign Ministers' Conference in Berlin decided to sponsor a conference in Geneva of the nine powers concerned with Indochina (the United States, the Soviet Union, Britain, France, Laos, Cambodia, the Viet Minh, led by Ho, the Bao Dai regime, which was the client of France in southern Vietnam, and China). The Geneva Agreements, concluded in the summer of 1954, established a cease-fire line at approximately the 17th parallel, behind which both sides would withdraw their military forces, the French to the south, the Viet Minh to the north. The French were to regroup for eventual withdrawal, and by 1956 a general election throughout all of Vietnam would be held to decide on a unified government.

The 17th parallel did *not* constitute a division of the country into two parts. Chapter one, article 1, of the Geneva Agreements reads, "A *provisional* military demarcation line shall be fixed, on either side of which the forces of the two parties shall be regrouped after their withdrawal" [emphasis added]. Section 6 of the final declaration stated that "The military demarcation line is provisional and should not in any way be interpreted as constituting a political or territorial boundary."[17]

Other important articles of the Agreements included:

Article 16: The introduction into Viet-Nam of any troop reinforcements and additional military personnel is prohibited.

Article 17: The introduction into Viet-Nam of any reinforcements in the form of all types of arms, munitions and war matériel, such as combat aircraft, naval craft, pieces of ordnance, jet engines and jet weapons, and armoured vehicles, is prohibited.

Article 18: The establishment of new military bases is prohibited throughout Viet-Nam territory.

Article 19: No military base under the control of a foreign State may be established in the regrouping zone of either party.[18]

The United States did not sign the final declaration at Geneva, and America's delegate, Under-Secretary of State Walter B. Smith, declared:

With regard to the aforesaid agreements and paragraphs that (1) it will refrain from the threat or the use of force to disturb them, in accordance with Article 2 [4] of the Charter of the United Nations dealing with the obligation of members to refrain in their international relations from the threat or use of force; and (2) it would view any renewal of aggression in violation of the aforesaid agreements with grave concern and as seriously threatening international peace and security.[19]

The elections of 1956 called for in the Agreements were never held.

NOTES

1. Truong Buu Lam, *Patterns of Vietnamese Response to Foreign Intervention: 1858–1900*, Monograph Series No. 11, Southeast Asia Studies (New Haven: Yale University Press, 1967).

2. George McTurnan Kahin and John W. Lewis, *The United States in Vietnam* (New York: Dell, 1967), pp. 10–14.

3. Ibid., p. 29.

4. U.S. Cong., House, *United States-Vietnam Relations*, 1945–1967: Study Prepared by the Department of Defense, 12 vols. (Washington, D.C.: GPO, 1971), 1: A-11, A-12, A-13.

5. Ibid., p. A-20.

6. Quoted in Richard E. Ward, "The Origins of U.S. Intervention in Vietnam," *Vietnam Quarterly*, no. 1 (Winter 1976), p. 8.

7. Kahin and Lewis, pp. 15–17.

8. Ward, p. 8.

9. Quoted in Noam Chomsky, "From Mad Jack to Mad Henry," *Vietnam Quarterly*, no. 1 (Winter 1976), p. 17.

10. Kahin and Lewis, pp. 23, 24.

11. Philippe Devillers, "'Supporting' the French in Indochina?," in *The Pentagon Papers: Critical Essays*, eds. Noam Chomsky and Howard Zinn, GE V, 163. This is the Senator Gravel Edition, *The Pentagon Papers: The Defense Department History of United States Decisionmaking on Vietnam*, 5 vols. (Boston: Beacon Press, 1972), hereafter cited as *The Pentagon Papers*, GE.

12. Kahin and Lewis, pp. 26, 27.

13. *The Pentagon Papers*, GE, I: 22, 47.

14. Devillers, p. 164.

15. The New York *Times*, April 7, 1954.

16. Quoted in U.S. Cong., Senate, *Causes, Origins and Lessons of the Vietnam War*, 92nd Cong., 2nd sess. (Washington, D.C.: GPO, 1973), p. 169.

17. The Geneva Agreements on the Cessation of Hostilities in Viet Nam, July 20, 1954.

18. Ibid.

19. Ibid.

5

The Diem Years: 1954-63

THE EMERGENCE OF NGO DINH DIEM

In an effort to subvert the Geneva Agreements and block the impending victory of Ho Chi Minh in the 1956 elections, the United States placed its hopes in one man, Ngo Dinh Diem. Diem was a Catholic and anti-Communist, a mandarin who had worked in the French imperial administration in the early 1930s. In 1933, however, he resigned over a dispute with Emperor Bao Dai and spent the next thirteen years secluded from political life. In 1946 he attempted to organize political opposition to Ho and the Viet Minh but was unsuccessful and left Vietnam for a four-year exile, mostly in the United States where he attempted to gather support from intellectual, political, and religious leaders. He returned to Vietnam in 1954 and was named Premier of the French client regime headed by Bao Dai.[1] Diem had gone to the United States at the urging of Professor Wesley Fishel, whom he met in Toyko during his exile. Fishel was to later head the Michigan State University-CIA group in Saigon.[2]

Little can be understood about Diem and his regime outside the context of the Nhu family, which was woven entirely into the regime's fabric. Diem's sister-in-law, Madame Nhu, was presidential hostess for the regime, a member of the National Assembly, and head of the Women's Solidarity Movement. Diem's brother Ngo Dinh Nhu was his right hand man and adviser and reputed to be the power behind the Diem presidency. His brother Ngo Dinh Can was virtual ruler of the Annam region, and his brother Ngo Dinh Thuc, Archbishop of Hue and Primate of South Vietnam, was also a presidential adviser. A fourth brother, Ngo Dinh Luyen, became an ambassador. Three family members served in the first cabinet and two in-laws held key positions as Secretary of State and Assistant Secretary for National Defense.[3] Madame Nhu's father was "the American's trusted man in Saigon" and Ambassador to Washington until August 1963, when he resigned over the regime's treatment of the Buddhists.[4] Diem himself trusted only personal acquaintances for high office, once having remarked that "Society . . . functions through personal relations among men at the top."[5]

Widespread graft and corruption characterized the Diem regime. Vietnamese officials followed the example of the French and deposited funds in France as a safeguard against political changes. One province chief stated that in the struggle against the Viet Minh it was most important to have strong officials who could control them; personal honesty and competence were not as important. As he stated, "It is better to have a district chief who steals than a district full of Communists." The Vietnamese who aided the French occupation continued their graft and corruption in the post-Geneva period, to the point that even Diem described it "as reaching the proportions of a 'social plague'" in the South.[6]

Diem's first major conflict began in February 1955 with various religious sects (not including the Buddhists) who held political power. These sects included gangsters and river pirates who controlled Saigon prostitution, gambling, and the police force, and had private, French-subsidized armies. The various sects joined together to form a united front against Diem and called for an end to his power as Premier, but he refused to relinquish his power. Finally, in March and April 1955, Diem's troops broke the opposition.[7]

Diem actually took complete power in South Vietnam through a national referendum held in October 1955 on the issue of monarchy versus a republic. Diem led the republican forces against Bao Dai, who was considered a symbol of the discredited French-supported monarchy. Regarding this election, Bernard Fall, scholar-journalist who covered both the French and American wars in Vietnam, writes:

All sources with any pretension to objectivity agree that Bao Dai was given very little opportunity to present his case to the voters. As [Donald] Lancaster, then a senior political officer at the British Embassy in Saigon, observed: "The campaign was conducted with such cynical disregard for decency and democratic principles that even the Viet Minh professed to be shocked."[8]

In nearly all areas the number of yes votes cast exceeded the number of voters, and in the Saigon area 605,000 votes were cast by 450,000 registered voters.[9] By January 1956 the Revolutionary Committee that had been set up to conduct the election was disbanded and most of its members were forced into exile. The election was followed by a general-assembly election in March, 1956; but of the 123 members elected, not one belonged to the "loyal opposition."[10] Assistant Secretary of State Walter Robertson, however, called the balloting "eloquent testimony to the new state of affairs," for the voice of the people had been expressed "by an overwhelming majority for President Diem's leadership."[11] In this and subsequent elections, Diem would suppress his opposition, with the press "closely muzzled" and then finally shut down.[12]

It was during this early period that Diem established his power, "against French advice . . . but with almost unwavering support" from Secretary of State John Foster Dulles.

His "anti-communist moralism" made any conciliation with the DRV impossible, and this ensured that the temporary 17th parallel established by the Geneva Agreements would become a permanent division between North and South Vietnam.[13]

THE DIEM REGIME, THE UNITED STATES, AND THE GENEVA AGREEMENTS

Just prior to the opening of the Geneva Conference, which would negotiate an end to the French-Indochinese conflict, the United States National Security Council (NSC) had supported recommendations rejecting a cease-fire and the establishment of a coalition government. The NSC also supported a Department of Defense report stating that if the French accepted a negotiated settlement at Geneva that harmed American interests in Indochina, "the U.S. should decline to associate itself with such a settlement and should pursue . . . ways and means of continuing the struggle against the Viet Minh."[14] The report also recommended that the United States support political and covert action that would "make every possible effort, *not openly inconsistent* with the U.S. position as to the armistice agreements, to defeat Communist subversion and influence," and it urged the United States to work through the French "only insofar as necessary" for "internal security" and to "exploit every available means to make more difficult control by the Viet Minh of North Vietnam."[15]

While the nine nations were meeting in Geneva, the United States was using a CIA team to sabotage key installations in Vietnam that were to be turned over to the Viet Minh. By June 1, 1954, Colonel Edward Lansdale of the CIA had arrived in Saigon to direct "paramilitary operations against the enemy and to wage political-psychological warfare." After the Geneva Agreements were signed, this mission was "modified to prepare the means for undertaking paramilitary operations in Communist areas rather than to wage unconventional warfare."[16]

Just before the signing of the Agreements, the Lansdale group contaminated the oil supply of a bus company, took first actions toward delayed sabotage of railroads and compiled detailed notes of potential targets for future operations. "The sabotage of the bus company was specifically aimed at the French concept of economic co-existence with the Democratic Republic of Vietnam (DRV), the bus company being owned and staffed by French personnel."[17] These activities would continue, and by the close of the Conference "the first of . . . an endless flow of American advisers, researchers and intelligence agents had reached Saigon."[18] The Conference changed little so far as the United States was concerned. Jean Chauvel, head of the French delegation at Geneva, stated that "the only purpose of the Geneva Agreements, as [the Americans] see them, is to provide a cover for the political, economic, and military preparations for the conquest."[19]

In the official American view the Agreements had been "a disaster for the free world" because they gave the North Vietnamese and Chinese a "new base for exploitation of Southeast Asia" and "enhanced Peking's prestige to Washington's dismay and detriment." The NSC met in August 1954 to summarize the conference and to prepare various proposals for covert operations and other efforts to block the substance and spirit of the Agreements.[20] Noam Chomsky, a professor at the Massachusetts Institute of Technology and author of a number of articles and books on the Vietnam War, argues that this meeting actually set the ground rules for future U.S. intervention by indicating that Washington would view any rebellion or subversion to a "legitimate government" as an invitation for both covert support and, with congressional approval, the possible use of military forces. Chomsky points out that this "doctrine is in clear and explicit violation of the law." In essence it said that the U.S. is not bound by its fundamental obligations under the United Nations Charter. . . . Since the "legitimacy" of a local government is a matter of unilateral [American] decision, the statement implies that the United States will intervene as it sees fit in the internal affairs of other countries.[21]

These secret policies were formulated in spite of the public declaration issued at Geneva regarding the use of force or the threat of force to disturb the Agreements.

In a letter to John F. Kennedy in 1961, when he appealed to the President for assistance in defending his regime against North Vietnamese "aggression," Diem stated that the Communists had "never ceased to violate the Geneva Agreements." From the beginning they had "resorted to terror in their efforts to subvert our people, destroy our government, and impose a Communist regime upon us."[22] These statements were simply untrue. Terror and violence were the first and central aspects of the Diem regime, and it was this systematic terrorism that was the principal violation of the Agreements. Joseph Buttinger, a former Diem adviser and supporter, describes the terrorism that occurred during the early post-Geneva period:

In June 1956 Diem organized two massive expeditions into regions that were controlled by the Communists without the slightest use of force. His soldiers arrested tens of thousands of people. . . . Hundreds, perhaps thousands of peasants were killed. Whole villages whose populations were not friendly to the government were destroyed by artillery. These facts were kept secret from the American people.[23]

Further, he points out that in these manhunts

there can be no doubt . . . that innumerable crimes and absolutely senseless acts of suppression against both real and suspected Communists were committed. . . . Most of the real Communists escaped and judging by the treatment the South Vietnamese army later accorded to captured guerrillas, most likely also were tortured.[24]

Jeffrey Race, a former U.S. army adviser in South Vietnam who had access to U.S. and Saigon intelligence files and was one of the few Americans who understood and spoke Vietnamese, also confirms this view. Race states that the government manhunts destroyed "almost the entire political apparatus the [Viet Minh] had concealed in the South." The Agreements specifically forbade any reprisals against former resistance fighters, but the Diem regime "employed every means to track them down and arrest them. . . . After arrest, the cadres would be liquidated."[25] Race interviewed a National Assembly candidate who said: "Everyone was terrified of the government. . . ." (Was there torture?) "Of course there was. . . . But there was nothing anyone could do. Everyone was too terrified."[26] It was in reaction to this terrorism that armed struggle and resistance in the South resumed. Diemist policies, with U.S. support, made it an inevitable development.

Another aspect of this early terrorism was the "Denounce Communists" campaign, which was marked by political suppression against former Viet Minh cadres and their supporters. The regime held mass meetings throughout the country in an attempt to get people to inform on the Viet Minh and other political dissidents, and also urged former Viet Minh guerrillas to join the regime and abandon their former comrades.

According to official estimates, 20,000–30,000 former Viet Minh cadres were put into concentration camps (most observers believe the number to be considerably higher), but P. J. Honey [a leading apologist for the regime], whose anti-Communist record was well known, had occasion to visit these camps. He reported that "the majority of the detainees are neither Communist nor pro-Communist."[27]

The United States actively supported this campaign through the Michigan State University–CIA police effort, which aided the regime by training, equipping and financing Diem's civil militia and police force. The Michigan State group trained authorities to fingerprint and maintain dossiers on political opponents, and supplied the militia and police with weaponry, ammunition and military vehicles.[28] *The Pentagon Papers* conclude that whatever the campaign "contributed to internal GVN security . . . [it] thoroughly terrified the . . . peasants, and detracted significantly from the regime's popularity."[29] By 1958 the round-up of those opposed to the regime had become frequent and brutal. Villages would be encircled while searches and raids took place, ending in arrests of suspects, interrogations, torture, deportation, and regrouping.[30] The South Vietnamese Minister of Information admitted that the "number of enemies 'eliminated' by the Baon militia" was 21,600 from 1955 to 1960.[31]

The knowledge that Diem was running such a terrorist state was known to Western and U.S. analysts. William Henderson, assistant executive director of the Council on Foreign Relations, wrote in *Foreign Affairs* five months before Diem's 1957 visit to the U.S.: "From the beginning Diem had ruled virtually as a dictator. South Vietnam was a quasi-police state characterized by arbitrary arrests and imprisonment, strict censorship of the press and the absence of effective political opposition."[32] David Hotham, correspondent in South Vietnam for the London *Times* and *The Economist* in 1955–57, made the following observations:

The West is backing, with its eyes open . . . a reactionary police state. . . . The Asians are intelligent people, and well able to contrast the declaration of principles of . . . the United States, with the facts of the regime under which they live. No intelligent Vietnamese can fail to be cynical when he hears American professors lecturing of political freedom in one province, while Diem's army and police are imprisoning thousands of suspected Communists without trial in another.[33]

By late 1957 newspapers critical of regime policies were being harassed, and in March 1958 the largest paper in

Saigon was closed down. In 1958 opposition candidates risked arrest for trying to form unauthorized parties, and by 1959 "all political opposition activity had come to a halt."[34] By the fall of 1960 the intellectual elite was silent, the labor unions were impotent, and opposing organized parties did not exist. "Diem's policies virtually assured that political challenges to him would be extra-legal. Ultimately these emerged . . . from the armed forces, the religious sects, and the armed peasantry."[35]

In April 1960, 18 prominent political leaders, including 11 former cabinet ministers, issued a public letter to Diem. They stated that they could not

remain indifferent to the realities of life in our country. . . . Continuous arrests fill the jails and prisons to the rafters, as at this precise moment, public opinion and the press are reduced to silence. . . . Political parties and religious sects have been eliminated. . . . The people today want freedom. . . . Sources of revenue are in the hands of speculators who use the [government] party . . . for certain private interests. . . . The government . . . should put an end to all forms of human exploitation in the [work camps].[36]

All were eventually jailed or exiled after the declaration.

Arthur Schlesinger, historian and former Kennedy adviser, writes that "Diem's authoritarianism, which increasingly involved manhunts, political reeducation camps and the 'regroupment' of populations, caused spreading discontent and then armed resistance in the countryside."[37] *The Pentagon Papers* note:

Enough evidence has now been accumulated to establish that peasant resentment against Diem was extensive and well founded. Moreover, it is clear that the dislike of the Diem government was coupled with resentment toward Americans. For many peasants the War of Resistance against French-Bao Dai rule never ended; France was merely replaced by the U.S., Bao Dai's mantle was transferred to . . . Diem.[38]

Joseph Kraft, Washington correspondent who wrote the introduction to Jean Lacouture's *Vietnam: Between Two Truces*, states that the former Viet Minh were very disciplined and did not "initiate trouble" against the regime, but others oppressed by the regime were not so disciplined and had no concerns about repercussions for the DRV. Thus Communists were pressured to act, and others who did resist inevitably looked to the Communists and former Viet Minh for support. "In short, like almost all rebellions, the . . . revolt was not set off by some master planner. . . . It was generated basically by local conditions."[39] Jeffrey Race supports Kraft's view, stating that in the period following the Geneva Agreements former Viet Minh guerrillas and supporters engaged in peaceful political activity in preparation for the 1956 elections. They took an "almost entirely defensive role during this period"; this defensive posture, however, almost destroyed their political organization as the Diem regime took an increasingly violent and offensive stand against all political opponents. The violence of the regime finally left the Viet Minh and other political dissidents no alternative but armed struggle against Diem's suppression.[40]

The terrorism of the Diem regime in this post-Geneva period was obscured by the propaganda about the hundreds of thousands of refugees who left North Vietnam after the signing of the Agreements. *The Pentagon Papers* state that the refugee movement from the North was important because it provided "the earliest convincing evidence of the undemocratic and oppressive nature of the North Vietnamese regime"; it "engaged the sympathies of the American people as few developments in Vietnam have before or since and solidly underwrote the U.S. decision for unstinting support of Diem"; and the Catholic refugees "provided Diem with a . . . politically malleable, culturally distinct group, wholly distrustful of Ho Chi Minh and the DRV, dependent for subsistence" on his government.[41]

Jean Lacouture, a French journalist who has written

extensively on Vietnamese affairs, calls the refugee issue "one triumph" for Diem's regime—"the integration of nearly a million refugees from the North."

However one may judge the reasons that led . . . hundreds of thousands of men—mostly Christians—to leave their . . . villages . . . one must appreciate what was done for them in [the South]. It will be said, of course, that the credit goes to American money and to the activity of the Catholic clergy. Still the Diem state was able to coordinate the necessary efforts with great diligence.[42]

Eisenhower sent a letter to Diem on October 23, 1954, in which he referred to the request of aid to "assist . . . the movement of several hundred thousand loyal Vietnamese citizens away from areas which are passing under a de facto rule and political ideology which they abhor." He said he was "glad that the U.S. [could] assist in this humanitarian effort."[43] Tom Dooley, a Navy doctor working in South Vietnam, and Cardinal Spellman, aroused American pity for, in Spellman's words, the "diseased, mutilated Asians fleeing from the Godless cruelties of communism . . . thousands of evacuees fleeing from Communist terror."[44] At the 1954 American Legion convention, Spellman also called for the destruction of Ho's revolution, "else we shall risk bartering our liberties for lunacies, betraying the sacred trust of our forefathers, becoming serfs and slaves to Red rulers' Godless goons." He asked the Legionnaires to "pray for God's intervention . . . lest we forget and surrender to those who have attacked us without cause, those who have repaid us with evil for good and hatred for love.[45] Bernard Fall placed the number of Catholic refugees moving South at between 500,000 and 600,000. These refugees "became the political shock troops of the regime, providing the cheering crowds that for so long fooled American official visitors about the popularity of Diem and the 'safe constituencies' which unfailingly elected regime-approved candidates by 99 per cent majorities."[46]

The refugee myth was perhaps the most important one

put forth by the "Vietnam Lobby," a group of American anti-Communist intellectual, political, and religious leaders who formed in support of Diem and told the American people about the "miracle of democracy" flowering in South Vietnam. This was accomplished through favorable media coverage, political connections between the Lobby, Congress (which included Lobby members) and the Eisenhower Administration, and organized public relations campaigns designed to package Diem and his regime. The refugees were settled and cared for through extensive aid from the United States and the Catholic Relief Agency, and they became a "privileged minority and source of support" for Diem. Most of the refugees came from two heavily Catholic provinces, and priests aided this flow by telling them that "God and the Virgin Mary have gone South; only the devil remains in the North." They manufactured atrocity stories, aided in this endeavor by CIA agents. Through his books and articles, radio and television appearances, and talks to civic, fraternal and religious groups, Dooley convinced Americans that the "flight of the refugees represented condemnation of the Viet Minh by the bulk of the Vietnamese population." He spoke of the oppression of Catholics, implying that their grievances were general to the population, thus giving the impression that "we were helping a whole people on the path to *their* freedom when for better or worse they wanted to travel the other way."[47]

Chomsky challenges the view stated by Leslie Gelb in *The Pentagon Papers* that this refugee flight "provided the world the earliest evidence of the undemocratic and oppressive nature of North Vietnam's regime," writing that "it is patently absurd to point to this flight as 'convincing evidence,'" for many of the Catholic refugees had been "collaborators and had even been mobilized into 'an autonomous Vietnamese militia against the Vietminh.'" He concludes: "Would one argue that the flight of Loyalists to Canada provided the world with the earliest convincing evidence of the undemocratic and oppressive nature of . . . [George] Washington's regime?"[48]

Despite the American and South Vietnamese charge that the North Vietnamese were guilty in the post-Geneva period of massive violations of the Agreements, the 6th Interim Report of the International Control Commission (ICC), which was set up to monitor the Agreements, stated: "While the Commission has experienced difficulties in North Vietnam, the major part of its difficulties has arisen in South Vietnam."[49] One analyst concluded that the "Vietminh regime in the north, for its part, eagerly welcomed the Commission, and as the documents . . . show, generally cooperated."[50]

The key event during the post-Geneva period was to be the national elections for reunification stipulated by the Agreements, scheduled to be held in July 1956. The official U.S. view maintained that there could be no free elections in the North under Ho Chi Minh, and thus Diem was wise not to trust the Communists.

Before and after the Geneva Conference the National Security Council rejected any notion of self-determination through free elections, arguing that it was "infeasible and such a course of action would, in any case, lead to the loss of [Vietnam] to Communist control."[51] *The Pentagon Papers* report that this NSC objective "did *not* connote American intervention to subvert the [Agreements]; read in context, the phrase meant that American influence would aim at assuring that the Communists not gain an electoral victory through deceitful, undemocratic methods in violation of the Final Declaration's stipulation that they be 'free.'"[52]

The Pentagon historians attempted to impute pure motives to the United States where none existed. Even U.S. intelligence sources made it clear that if the all-Vietnam elections were held in an open and free manner, Ho Chi Minh would win overwhelmingly. And, in April 1955, a Department of Defense report concluded that if the Viet Minh allowed the elections under international supervision, "there is no reason to doubt . . . they would win easily."[53] This was known to U.S. officials before, during, and after the Geneva Conference; thus they were faced with the choice of

Viet Minh control of Vietnam, or subversion and terrorism in support of an American-imposed regime to prevent this reality.

The myth was fostered that the Diem regime sought reunification of Vietnam and attempted continually to meet with the DRV to discuss the elections. Diem stated that his government had "always been prepared and on many occasions stated our willingness to reunify Viet-Nam on the basis of democratic and truly free elections."[54] Secretary Robertson supported this position, arguing that Diem and his government had reaffirmed a

desire to seek the reunification of Vietnam by peaceful means. . . . We support them fully. . . . For our part we believe in free elections, and we support President Diem fully in his position that there first must be conditions which preclude intimidation or coercion of the electorate. Unless such conditions exist there can be no free choice.[55]

Another myth fostered was that "free elections for all Vietnam . . . was simply a means of enslaving the free people of Vietnam. . . . The Communist-backed Viet Minh would almost certainly win, because they had 'duped' the populace." The United States was "saving" the South Vietnamese from themselves, "teaching them . . . American democracy through Diem's 'showcase' government."[56]

Throughout this period the Viet Minh tried numerous times, unsuccessfully, to get the Diem regime to carry out the Geneva provisions for consultations leading up to the actual elections. *The Pentagon Papers* state that "The French urgently sought to persuade Diem to accept consultations about the elections. . . . Britain [also] . . . joined France in urging Diem to talk to the Vietminh." But Diem refused.[57] He was supported in this refusal by the United States, for he could not have balked had Washington supported the Agreements. In addition to French and British pressures, on six occasions from May 1956 to July 1960, the DRV suggested to Diem that preelection consultations be held; they offered to "negotiate on the basis of 'free general elections by secret ballot.' Each time it met with scornful silence or stinging replies."[58]

Jean Lacouture states that the Diem regime, believing that the elections in 1956 "could benefit only the North, made every effort to prevent any development in that direction, to discourage any such attempt, and to repress all conceivable initiative that could lead to reunification."[59] *The Pentagon Papers* note that Diem could not meet with the Viet Minh because this "would give the appearance of having accepted" the Agreements. He refused to "'consider any proposal from the Communists' without proof that they had mended their ways and were prepared to hold genuinely free elections." As the deadline approached, Diem came to the view that free elections were not possible in North Vietnam, and he had "no intention of consulting with the DRV concerning them." The Pentagon historians allege that Washington "did not . . . connive with Diem" to block the elections. The United States acquiesced because of Diem's opposition, and "evidence then accumulated about the oppressive nature of the regime in North Vietnam."[60]

Despite the apologetics of the Pentagon historians, it is eminently clear that Diem could not have refused to hold the elections without U.S. support; thus the United States was complicit in their not being held in 1956. After-the-fact statements about Diem's opposition, and the oppressive nature of the DRV regime, are merely rationalizations to hide the essential truth. George McTurnan Kahin discusses the fundamental issues surrounding the elections and the implications of their cancellation:

In mid-1955 . . . Diem—with U.S. encouragement—announced that the elections . . . would not be held. Regardless of what sophistry has been employed . . . in encouraging this move the U.S. reneged on its own declaration . . . at Geneva. . . . Until 1958 the Hanoi government persisted in its efforts to arrange discussion for the promised elections, but Diem, consistently backed by the U.S., refused . . . having chosen not to carry out the heart of the Geneva

Agreements, Diem made civil war inevitable. For when a military struggle . . . ends on the agreed condition that the competition will be transferred to the political level, the side which repudiates the agreed conditions can hardly expect that the military struggle will not be resumed.[61]

All of the subsequent developments during the Diem era, including the rise of the National Liberation Front and the growing involvement of the United States, are intimately tied to the failure of the Diem regime and the United States to uphold that provision of the Geneva Agreements which called for elections throughout Vietnam.

In 1956, little known to the American people, Diem abolished elections for municipal councils because he feared large numbers of Viet Minh might win office. This ended some 500 years of traditional administrative authority of villages, which even under the French had enjoyed autonomy in most local civil matters, such as disputes, taxation, and managing public funds. Members of the village council and the chief were now appointed from Saigon directly by the regime.[62]

In 1959 the regime held its only attempted democratic election, but it proved embarrassing. Of course it was a democratic election, without the major opposition force, the Viet Minh, who had been driven underground by continued and massive violence directed against its members and supporters. Jeffrey Race interviewed a national assembly candidate in the election of 1959. "The . . . election was very dishonest. [Diem personnel] went around . . . and stuffed the ballot boxes. If the results didn't come out they were adjusted at district headquarters."[63] Official police records show that in one district that had been a Communist stronghold, the regime candidate received about 7,500 votes, while the opposition candidate polled 66.[64]

SUPPRESSION LEADS TO REVOLUTION

One of the major concerns of the Vietnamese peasants was land ownership and land reform, and Diem's record here was merely another factor that fueled the revolutionary movement against his regime. To some, Diem's land-reform program appeared to be progressive. However, "it meant the return of the landlord" (many of whom had openly or implicitly aided the French), and the peasants had to pay rent to purchase land they had already received from the Viet Minh.[65] Diem had hired a former New Deal adviser to study land reform, and this "convinced many American liberals" that he was serious. What actually happened is that the peasants lost land they already had.[66]

Robert Scigliano, who worked in South Vietnam in 1957–59 with the Michigan State Vietnam Advisory Group, summarizes the land-reform program:

The land transfer program was inadequate . . . in requiring the peasants to pay in full for land they were to receive. . . . Landlords in much of South Vietnam had virtually ceased to exercise their proprietary rights against squatters and tenants during the Indo-china War, and Communist agitation fed the peasants' belief that the land they occupied was theirs by right. . . . Finally, the number of people who lost and gained land under the program was not large. . . . Of an estimated 1 to 1.2 million tenant households existing in 1955, about ten percent obtained land under the . . . transfer program. . . .

That peasant dissatisfaction with land reform has been a breeding ground for the growth of Communist power in . . . Vietnam would seem indisputable.[67]

And *The Pentagon Papers* report:

Diem's [land] reform package compared unfavorably even in theory with what the Viet Minh had done. . . . By 1959, [it] was virtually inoperative. As of 1960, 45% of the land remained concentrated in the hands of 2% of landowners and 15% of the landlords owned 75% of all the land. Those relatively few farmers who did benefit from the program were most often than not northerners, refugees, Catholics . . . so that land reform added to the aura of favoritism which deepened peasant alienation. . . . Tensions were further aggravated by rumors of corruption, and the widespread allegation that the Diem family itself had become enriched through manipulation of land transfers.[68]

The pacification program was another crucial element in the regime's suppression of the peasantry. The program was devised by American advisers and British guerrilla-warfare expert Robert Thompson; it included strategic hamlets that were set up to provide protection for the villagers at night in an attempt to separate them from the Viet Cong. It was the regime's answer to the NLF strategy: "Strategic hamlets seek to insure the security of the people in order that the success of the political, social and military revolution might be assured by the enthusiastic movement of solidarity and self-sufficiency." Diem said that the plan was intended to "give back to the hamlet the right of self-government with its own charter and system of community law. This will realize the ideas of the constitution on a local scale the people can understand."[69]

However, the program was similar if not identical to earlier French efforts: "All failed dismally because they ran into resentment if not active resistance by peasants at whose control and safety, then loyalty, they were aimed." Diem and Nhu emphasized control of the peasants "as a precondition to winning loyalty," but they paid "scant attention" to past conditions.[70] Instead, it antagonized the peasants because they were moved from ancestral lands and from family burial grounds.[71]

Bernard Fall examined two pacification efforts during this period both of which failed badly, because the regime

was totally unwilling to move with political and economic reforms absolutely essential to the success of the program. . . . Under pressure from Saigon to "produce results," local officials proclaimed hamlet completion figures totally out of line with reality and as earlier under French rule, the foreign experts tended to fall in line with the officially expressed optimism, until it became clear after the fall of the Diem regime . . . that a bare twenty percent of about 8,000 hamlets were truly viable and likely to be defended in case of a VC attack.[72]

Violence and terrorism were directed especially upon the rural population by the pacification effort. John Mc-Dermott, a war critic and university scholar, writes:

In a period of eight years the entire system of the countryside was destroyed. . . . [The] schemes proved to the people that Vietcong propaganda was accurate. Diem was a puppet. . . . Because he was under the control of the Americans he was willing to raze houses, destroy . . . shrines . . . tear up sacred burial grounds, and force . . . people into what a *Wall Street Journal* reporter called "concentration camps."[73]

The Dallas *Morning News* stated:

Supposedly the purpose of the fortified villages is to keep the Viet Cong out, but barbed wire denies entrance and exit. Vietnamese farmers are forced at gunpoint into these virtual concentration camps. Their homes, possessions and crops are burned. . . . The anti-communist Democratic party of South Vietnam told the ICC that decapitation, eviscerations and public display of murdered women and children are common.[74]

Despite the blatant brutality of the pacification effort, American officials supported it enthusiastically from the beginning.

Under Secretary of State George W. Ball, commented favorably on the progressive development of strategic hamlets . . . as a method of combatting insurgency and as a means of bringing the entire nation "under control of the government."[75]

And Secretary of Defense Robert MacNamara stated in July 1962 that it was the "backbone of President Diem's program for countering subversion directed against his state."[76]

The Pentagon historians contend that the "abortive" Strategic Hamlet Program did not offer enough evidence to decide that it was a failure. "One may say that the program was doomed by poor execution and the inability of the Nhu family to reform coupled with the inability of the U.S. to induce it to reform. The evidence does not warrant one to proceed further."[77]

The conclusions of the Pentagon historians stress the technical problems of the program and avoid any real judgment on its brutality. The issue thus becomes one of efficiency and poor execution rather than of the terroristic nature of the effort itself. As Chomsky points out: "The analysts in the Pentagon study generally exhibit a commitment to the ideological underpinning of U.S. policy and its specific aims."[78]

The corrupt and terroristic policies of the Diem regime were responsible for the development of the revolutionary movement in South Vietnam, led by the National Liberation Front (NLF); although the official view of the origins of the liberation effort was that the DRV ("Hanoi") had organized and directed the aggression against the democratic Diem regime. In 1961 the State Department issued its official White Paper entitled "A Threat to the Peace." Secretary of State Dean Rusk said that it documented the "elaborate program of subversion, terror and armed infiltration carried out under the direction of . . . Hanoi." It revealed, with "extensive documentation," how North Vietnam had sent "agents, military personnel, weapons and supplies" into the South, their efforts including kidnapping, assassinations, and armed attacks; that North Vietnam had repeatedly violated the Geneva Agreements, and thus South Vietnam justifiably needed U.S. aid to defend itself against this attack.[79] Walt Rostow, adviser to Presidents Kennedy and Johnson, argued that Hanoi decided to "launch" a guerrilla effort in 1960–61 because of Diem's "increasing success in stabilizing his rule and moving his country forward in the several preceding years." He later admitted, however, that there was "dissatisfaction with Diem's method of rule, with his lack of identification with his people," and that this had "been endemic for years." Despite this admission, he recommended that the United States tell Moscow to "use its influence with Ho Chi Minh to call his dogs off, mind his business and feed his people."[80] An official U.S. mission sent to South Vietnam in 1961 stated that the country was "under attack in a bitter, total struggle which involves its security as a free nation. Its enemy, the Viet Cong, is ruthless, resourceful and elusive. This enemy is supplied, reinforced and centrally directed by the international Communist apparatus operating through Hanoi."[81]

Even the Pentagon historians concede that "significant doubt remains" regarding the official view. Viet Minh who had remained in the South after the Geneva Agreements in 1954 testified that their "mission was political agitation for the holding of the election promised at Geneva." Although some "'wildcat' activity" occurred in 1957 and 1958, efforts were aimed at the "careful construction of an underground apparatus which, although it used assassination and kidnapping . . . avoided military operations."[82] However, the Pentagon historians avoid confronting the myth of DRV aggression by suggesting that "whether or not the rebellion . . . proceeded independently of, or even contrary to, directions from Hanoi through 1958, Hanoi moved thereafter to capture the revolution."[83]

Chomsky argues that the conclusions of the Pentagon historians on the origins of the conflict against Diem are based upon fabrication that relies on CIA and Saigon intelligence material. He writes of the "more subtle, and rather pervasive bias" of the Pentagon analyst who summarized the early Diem period and the development of the insurgency:

He . . . notes that "no direct links have been established between Hanoi and the perpetrators of rural violence" in the 1956–1959 period. . . . By the phrase "perpetrators of rural violence," he does not refer to . . . Diem and his associates, who organized massive expeditions to peaceful Communist-controlled regions, killing hundreds, perhaps thousands of peasants and destroying whole

villages . . . nor to the "vengeful acts" of the South Vietnamese
Army in areas where the Vietminh had withdrawn after Geneva,
"arbitrarily arresting, harassing, and torturing the population."[84]

In discussing the sustained terrorism that began immediately after Geneva and continued throughout this early
period, the same Pentagon analyst states: "At least through
1957, Diem and his government enjoyed marked success with
fairly sophisticated pacification programs in the countryside." He does concede that "Diem instituted 'oppressive
measures' such as the so-called 'political reeducation centers'
which 'were in fact little more than concentration camps for
the potential foes of the government.'"[85] Despite these
admissions, the Pentagon historians avoid the only rational
judgment on the development of the resistance against
Diem: It was a justified and necessary effort. The issue of
Hanoi's involvement was merely a smokescreen to avoid the
unpleasant judgment that condemned the U.S. support of
Diem.

Kahin and Lewis state that despite

U.S. policy assumptions, all available evidence shows that the
revival of the civil war in the South in 1958 was undertaken by
Southerners at their own—not Hanoi's—initiative. . . . Insurgency
activity against the Saigon government began in the South under
Southern leadership not as a consequence of any dictates from
Hanoi but contrary to Hanoi's injunctions.[86]

Captured documents and later interviews with prisoners
make it clear that guerrillas in the South felt that Hanoi had
been reluctant to authorize much agitation beyond political
action. The guerrillas were forced to move more actively
against Diem's suppression for fear of losing any support
among the peasants, who were becoming increasingly
militant in the face of growing attacks by the regime. One
NLF leader suggested that the resumption of the war was
"impossible to avoid." There was pressure from the grass
roots, and as one peasant said, "If you do not enter the
struggle we will turn away from you."[87]

Lacouture places the origin of the NLF at March 1960, when a group of "old resistance fighters" gathered and declared that the situation under Diem was "intolerable" and "called upon patriots to regroup with a view toward ultimate collective action." A ten-point program was issued in December 1960, which was a "mixture of incitement to social efforts that could have come from a religious paternalist regime, and violent denunciations of American Policy."[88] In the first NLF Congress, held in March 1962, the platform supported a neutral stance in foreign policy and the eventual reunification of the nation, with the "independence of South Vietnam," which would "establish relations with all countries, accept aid from all states having different political views and aim at forming a peace zone, including Laos and Cambodia."[89]

Eqbal Ahmad, a noted authority on revolutionary movements in the Third World, has critically dissected the "outside-agitator, terrorist, and subversion" thesis. The view that a guerrilla movement "can be controlled and commanded by a foreign or externally based government, ignores the organizational, psychological and political facts of revolutionary warfare." The key issue is the necessity of mass support; "winning and maintaining popular support remains the central objective." Political factors are paramount, and such support depends upon the "moral alienation of the masses from the existing government." It is not created by "conspiracy," but by social and historical conditions. The terror that is seen as the primary basis for support "does not constitute the main reason" for peasant support, its use being "highly selective."[90]

The terrorism argument has been used to convince people that only through assassination, kidnapping, and murder was the NLF able to subvert an otherwise stable and democratic government. This position is more fantasy in the minds of American officials and uncritical observers than part of social reality. Ahmad's observation exposes the bankrupt view of Rusk and others, who suggested that the

NLF "[had] no significant popular following," and that terror was its main avenue of support.

Guerrilla warfare requires a highly committed but covert civilian support which cannot be obtained at gunpoint. Only degenerate or defeated guerrillas have risked the loss of popular support by terrorizing civilians. . . . The outstanding feature of guerrilla training is the stress on scrupulously "correct and just" behavior toward civilians. . . . Guerrilla use of terror is sociologically and psychologically selective. It strikes those who are popularly identified as the "enemy of the people"—officials, landlords and the like.[91]

Bernard Fall discusses the nature of guerrilla warfare and the issue of terrorism and violence, and his views support Ahmad's analysis. He particularly stresses the vital importance of peasant support, which cannot be obtained through terror: "For civilian support is *the* essential element of a successful guerrilla operation. . . . The Communists have correctly identified as the central objective of a revolutionary war—and, in fact, its only worthwhile prize—the *human beings* who make up the nation under attack."[92]

Thus it took all the "technological proficiency" the United States and its supporters had to "make up for the woeful lack of popular support and political savvy of most of the regimes that the West has thus far sought to prop up."[93] Compared to NLF cadres, Diem appointees to village posts were seen as having little or no legitimacy to the peasants because they represented the hated regime. The guerrillas had "no problem" preparing people to accept the execution of such officials.[94]

[This] could even be considered . . . "productive." When Diem ended the 400-to 500-year tradition of the democratic election of village chiefs . . . he made . . . probably his most crucial mistake. He began making local appointments from Saigon, and these appointees—many of them outsiders—were met with open hostility from villagers. [The appointees] would often have to go outside the village . . . to sleep safely. The hard fact is that when the Viet Cong assassinated these men, the Viet Cong were given a Robin Hood halo by the villagers.[95]

One aspect of the regime's terrorism that has almost been completely ignored is that of the special treatment of women. Susan Brownmiller, author of an extensive social and historical study of rape, relates a discussion she had with Peter Arnett, Pulitzer-prize-winning reporter for the Associated Press in South Vietnam:

Arnett . . . told me that it was common knowledge among the Saigon Press Corps that the Vietcong . . . rarely committed rape. . . . "The Vietcong would publicize an execution for rape. . . . Rape was a serious crime for them. It was considered a serious political blunder to rape and loot. It just wasn't done."[96]

When this behavior is contrasted with the conduct of the regime forces it becomes clear why the "other side" was winning the "hearts and minds" of the people.

The truth of the matter is that the creation and growth of the revolutionary struggle in South Vietnam during the Diem regime, led by the NLF, was

the result of indigenous Southern opposition to an oppressive regime . . . that the support for the NLF [was] considerable, particularly among the peasantry, and certainly greater than the support . . . given the Saigon cliques . . . and that at each stage in this . . . conflict the total aid given to the NLF by North Vietnam has been [a] small fraction of the assistance provided the Saigon governments by the U.S.[97]

Because of these facts the United States was forced to invent the "aggression and subversion" thesis in order to obscure the true origins and support of the resistance against Diem, and ultimately against the United States.

THE EISENHOWER AND KENNEDY ADMINISTRATIONS AND THE DIEM REGIME

During the early post-Geneva period South Vietnam clearly emerged as a client regime that was supported only by massive U.S. aid. Direct U.S. involvement in the regime can be traced back to the famous letter sent to Diem by Eisenhower in October 1954, in which he indicated that they would explore ways of assistance, contingent upon the development of economic and political reforms. The French were upset with this letter, feeling that it was an effort to interfere in Vietnamese affairs and that it would be "exploited by Communist propaganda." They felt the letter was intended to build up Diem while forcing his opponents into line.[98]

In addition to economic assistance, the United States sent large amounts of military aid and weaponry to Diem's armed forces, in direct violation of the Agreements. Formal letters were exchanged in January 1955, and the United States assumed training of the army and its financial support.[99] From 1954 to 1956 the United States sent more than a half billion dollars in aid to the Diem regime, more than 60 percent of it military assistance; in 1957 and 1958, out of $260 million in aid, the army received $200 million.[100]

George McTurnan Kahin contends that the United States did not give a "blank check to whatever regime" was in power in South Vietnam, but rather just to Diem; it was a "limited qualified pledge of economic support. It was not in any sense a pledge of *military* support, something which was . . . absolutely forbidden under the *Geneva Agreements.*" This "cornerstone" of our future involvement "was simply an undertaking to explore ways and means of giving aid . . . to resist subversion or aggression. But . . . even this was to be subject" to Vietnamese efforts at reform.[101]

In 1956 United States policy toward South Vietnam was established as assisting "Free Viet Nam to develop a strong stable and constitutional government to enable Free Viet Nam to assert an increasingly attractive contrast to conditions in the present Communist zone."[102] Part of this assistance included a public relations firm to package Diem in the United States, when he made an "official visit" here in May 1957. He addressed a joint session of Congress and attended a breakfast with Cardinal Spellman. Mayor Robert Wagner of New York called him a "man to whom freedom is the very breath of life itself," and he was presented with the Admiral Byrd award for "inspired leadership in the cause of the free world." During this visit the Vietnam Lobby emphasized the "miracle" theme of his government, with land reform, political stability, refugee resettlement, and economic development. But it was more of a "miracle of public relations."[103]

The public relations effort continued throughout this period. The New York *Times* stated that "Thomas Jefferson would have no quarrel" with Diem's definition of democracy.[104] Eisenhower complimented him "on the remarkable achievements" of South Vietnam under his leadership since 1954."[105] And in 1959 the *New Leader* hailed Diem's "Democratic One Man Rule," disregarding the contradictions in that statement.[106] The view presented to the American people in this period was that Diem was a "strong and capable leader, firmly in command of his own house, leading his people into modern nationhood at a remarkable pace."[107]

Despite the public glow regarding the Diem regime, however, internal memoranda throughout this period—not shared with the American people—indicated serious reservations about the actual situation. A National Intelligence Estimate (NIE) report in October 1955 stated that "[the] most significant articulate political sentiments of the bulk of the population was antipathy for the French combined with a personal regard for Ho Chi Minh as the symbol of Vietnamese nationalism."[108] That same year another intelligence report noted "adverse political trends stemming from Diem's 'authoritarian role.'" The report stated further that "the over-accumulation of grievances among various groups and individuals may lead to the development of a nationalist opposition movement."[109] And in 1959 yet another intelligence report came to a similar conclusion, expressing grave concern about Diem's leadership.

The prospects for continued political stability hang heavily upon Diem and his ability to maintain firm control of the army and the police. The regime's efforts to insure internal security and its belief that an authoritarian government is necessary to handle the country's problems will result in a continued repression of potential opposition elements.[110]

By 1961 a State Department paper indicated that the situation was "grave"; public officials, military men, and citizens spoke of the deterioration and loss of confidence in Diem and his leadership of the nation. "Intrigue, nepotism and even corruption might be expected, for a time, if combined with efficiency and visible progress. When they accompany administrative paralysis and steady deterioration, they become intolerable."[111] The key concern, however, was always whether the performance of the regime was effective; that this efficiency reflected brutal and suppressive policies was never the issue. As long as things worked, little question was raised on the nature of the policies.

The Kennedy Administration told the American people that it too was responding to the urgent appeal of a brave and determined nation, an appeal that had been addressed to Kennedy in a letter from Diem. Kennedy answered this appeal in December 1961, telling Diem that the situation was well known in the United States and that he was "deeply disturbed by the assault" on Diem's nation. "Our indignation has mounted as the deliberate savagery . . . of assassination, kidnapping, and wanton violence became clear."[112] In October 1961, when Kennedy sent General Maxwell Taylor to South Vietnam on an important fact-finding mission, Ambassador Frederick Nolting cabled Taylor enroute that his "conversations with . . . Vietnamese in various walks of life show virtually unanimous desire for introduction of U.S. forces into Viet-Nam." This view was based upon "unsolicited remarks from cabinet ministers, National Assembly Deputies, University professors, students, shopkeepers, and oppositionists."[113] On the basis of such information, Taylor told Kennedy: "There can be no action so convincing of U.S. seriousness of purpose and hence so reassuring to the people and government of SVN . . . as the introduction of U.S. forces. . . . The views of indigenous and U.S. officials consulted . . . were unanimous on this point."[114] This vigorous action was needed in South Vietnam because if the country fell, it would be "exceedingly difficult if not impossible, to hold Southeast Asia. What will be lost is not merely a crucial piece of real estate, but the faith that the U.S. has the will and capacity to deal with the Communist offensive in that area."[115] Communist strategy was to gain control of Southeast Asia by "subversion and guerrilla war," and this goal "[was] well on the way to success in Vietnam."[116]

As the NLF resistance began to rout Diem forces in 1960 and 1961, the United States stepped in and escalated the conflict. In November 1961 John Kennedy had Secretary Rusk advise the regime that the United States was going to "join [it] in a sharply increased effort to avoid a further deterioration of the situation in SVN."[117] This increased effort included expanded military aid, U.S. equipment and personnel for reconnaissance, special intelligence, air-group support, and small naval craft. The United States would train Diem's Civil Guard and Self-Defense Corps (among the most brutal and corrupt of all the South Vietnamese armed forces), and it would provide equipment and personnel to improve the intelligence system. Also included in this increased aid were six C-123 defoliant planes, which would be used to spray poisonous herbicides.[118]

All of this escalation and aggression took place during the New Frontier days. As Chomsky points out: "Kennedy significantly increased U.S. aggression in Indochina, a fact that liberal historians try to ignore."[119] As early as May 1962, disguised as U.S. "advisers," helicopter units were flying offensive strikes against NLF strongholds and unarmed villages.[120] During the Kennedy Administration, the American public was led to believe that the conflict against the NLF was being won or wound down, although as the Diem coup came closer there were conflicting reports within the inner circles regarding the weaknesses of the regime and its inability to win the war. Robert McNamara, who testified before Congress in March 1962, stated that he was " 'optimistic' over prospects for U.S. success" and "encouraged at the progress the South Vietnamese are making." The U.S. was trying to "clean it up . . . terminating subversion, covert aggression and combat operations."[121] By late spring of 1962, "the military situation . . . showed hopeful signs of at last having turned . . . a corner. . . . Continuing favorable developments now held forth the promise of eventual success, and to many the end of the insurgency seemed in sight."[122] And at the Honolulu Conference in July 1962, McNamara "was told and believed that there had been 'tremendous progress ' in the previous six months." This was repeated at the April 1963 conference meeting; and even as late as July 1963, in the midst of the Buddhist crisis, intelligence reports were encouraging. However, the Bureau of Intelligence and Research, State Department (INR), felt that the pattern of military successes had revealed a "steady decline" in the previous months. But this was greeted with a "storm of disagreement and . . . disregarded."[123]

It was the political conflict between the Buddhists and the Diem regime that finally brought the true nature of the regime home to the American people. The conflict had been festering for some time, but it had not resulted in violent confrontation. Lacouture states that Diem did not treat the Buddhists cruelly before the crisis, but his "Catholic sectarianism led him to treat them as a minor factor and with distrust." The catalyst for the crisis was a demonstration on May 8, 1963, in Hué to protest Diem's decision not to allow a public ceremony in honor of Buddha's birthday. There had been huge processions two weeks earlier by Catholics when two bishops were installed, and another on the anniversary of Diem's brother Thuc becoming Archbishop.[124] The troops in Hué used guns and tear gas to disperse the crowds; nine people were killed. The regime reported that "a Viet

Cong agent had thrown a grenade into the crowd and that the victims had been crushed in a stampede. It steadfastly refused to admit responsibility even when neutral observers produced films showing government troops firing on the crowd."[125]

The following day some 10,000 people demonstrated against the regime, the first of a number of actions during the next four months. On May 10, the Buddhist clergy demanded the freedom to fly the Buddhist flag, "legal equality with the Catholic church, the end of arrests, the freedom to practice their beliefs, and indemnification of the victims . . . with punishment for its perpetrators." Diem did not respond. Demonstrations continued through May and June, and by then many in the cities had rallied to the Buddhist protest. On June 8, Madame Nhu declared that the Buddhists were "infiltrated by communists."[126] Under U.S. pressure a joint Buddhist—South Vietnamese agreement was announced on June 16, "outlining the elements of a settlement, but affixing no responsibility" for the killings. The next day, however, Diem's troops again used violence to suppress Buddhist protests, and conditions worsened.[127]

In July the regime announced that the committee investigating the May 8th incident decided that the deaths were the result of "Viet Cong terrorism." The Buddhists were outraged, denouncing the findings and expanding their protests. This militancy would reach new heights on August 5, 15, and 18 with the self-immolation of [several] monks and a nun.[128] On August 21, on direct orders from his brother Ngo Dinh Nhu, Diem's Special Forces raided Buddhist pagodas throughout South Vietnam. They arrested hundreds of monks, effectively destroying U.S. efforts at conciliation and "marking the beginning of the end of the Diem regime." Pagodas were sacked in all major cities and more than 1,400 Buddhists (mainly monks) were arrested. In one incident about 30 monks were injured or wounded and several were listed as missing. "[It] was never established whether [Diem] knew and approved of Nhu's plans for the pagoda raids. . . .

Significantly, he never subsequently sought to disassociate himself from Nhu or the raids."[129]

Reaction to the raids was dramatic. Madame Nhu's mother, an observer at the United Nations, and her father, Ambassador to Washington, both resigned. The Foreign Minister of South Vietnam also resigned, and as a symbol of protest he shaved his head like a monk. Students at the University of Saigon protested in support of the Buddhists. The regime responded with massive arrests, but the demonstrations continued, and the university was finally closed. Then the protest was joined by high-school and junior high-school students. A few monks "took refuge in the U.S. embassy, where they were warmly received by [Ambassador Henry Cabot] Lodge."[130] The Kennedy Administration was angered by Nhu's move against the pagodas. It was felt that he had maneuvered himself into a position of power, a situation the United States could not tolerate. "Diem must be given chance to get rid of Nhu and his coterie and replace them with best military and political personalities available. If . . . Diem remains obdurate and refuses then [perhaps] Diem himself cannot be preserved."[131]

This crisis deepened, however, even as the elections for the National Assembly were being held. After a perfunctory one-week campaign, the Diemist candidates (on the ballot alone or with few authorized opponents) won overwhelming victories. Diem played down the martial-law reality, blaming the Communists for the crisis, as well as "foreign adventurers, and the Western press."[132]

The Pentagon authors state that the crisis became "a vehicle for mobilizing widespread resentment of an arbitrary and often oppressive rule."[133]

No one then foresaw that it would generate a national opposition movement capable of rallying virtually all non-communist dissidence in South Vietnam. . . . No one then appreciated the degree of alienation of Vietnam's people from their government, nor the extent of political decay within the regime.[134]

They contend that "no real low-risk alternative to Diem had ever been identified and we had continued our support . . . because [he] was regarded as the only Vietnamese figure capable of rallying national support in the struggle against the Viet Cong." However, the "Buddhist crisis shattered our illusions about him, and increased the domestic U.S. political price to Kennedy of supporting Diem."[135]

Kennedy drafted a letter on the Buddhist crisis, but it was to be used only if the situation became serious enough to warrant direct U.S. pressure. It was a "harsh, blunt" letter which stated that unless the regime changed its suppressive policies and methods and gained broader popular support, the United States might have to consider dissociating itself, with further aid perhaps impossible. McNamara and Lodge strongly recommended that the letter not be sent. They agreed that the situation was serious, but that it would not likely be changed by such a letter. It was never sent.[136]

The crisis continued as the United States began working with South Vietnamese generals toward the coup against Diem, which came some three weeks later. The culminating event of the Diem years was his assassination, ending his rule in South Vietnam. The official view being given to the American people was one of increasing concern with the Diem regime, but this did not reflect decisions that gave the green light to those military officers attempting to over-throw Diem.

The Kennedy Administration's involvement was in direct contrast to the official view presented to the people, that of a unified policy. Instead, the internal differences between U.S. policy-makers on the fate of the Diem regime were marked. In August two Administration officials argued that the United States "should not continue [its] support of a Nhu-dominated regime because its repressive tactics would eventually have a disastrous effect on the war." Both McNamara and Taylor were unconvinced and asked for "evidence" of this assertion.[137] Paul Kattenburg of the State Department

estimated that the United States "would be thrown out of the
country within six months if the regime remained in power"
and that the United States should be considering how "to get
out honorably." Dean Rusk challenged this view and said
that U.S. policy had to proceed on two basic assumptions:
that the United States would neither pull out until the war
was won nor "run a coup."[138]

The Pentagon Papers report that "the U.S. must accept its
full share of responsibility" for the Diem coup, for beginning in August 1963 Washington "authorized, sanctioned
and encouraged the coup efforts."[139] On October 5, the
Kennedy Administration suspended approval of AID loans
for a waterworks and electric-power project, and it suspended support of the South Vietnamese Special Forces
(which guarded Diem and the Presidential Palace) unless
they were transferred to the field under joint command
authority.[140] The regime reacted strongly to this through its
mouthpiece, the *Times of Vietnam*, which "accused the U.S.
of subverting the war effort and asserted that the cut-off had
been decided in mid-September." It concluded that "fan-
tastic pressures for petty reforms would jeopardize the entire
revolutionary program of the government."[141] Kennedy sent
a telegram to Lodge on October 5, indicating the new course
of action toward the Diem regime:

Actions are designed to indicate to Diem government our dis-
pleasure at its political policies and actions to create significant
uncertainty in that government and in key Vietnamese groups as to
future intentions of the United States. At the same time actions are
designed to have at most slight impact on military or counter-
insurgency effort against Viet Cong, at least in short term.[142]

Lodge had urged all-out support for the coup in a cable to
Kennedy:

We are launched on a course from which there is no respectable
turning back: The overthrow of the Diem government. There is
no turning back in part because US prestige is already publically
committed to this end in large measure and will become more so as

facts leak out. . . . There is no turning back because there is no possibility . . . that the war can be won under a Diem administration, still less that Diem or any member of the family can govern the country in a way to gain the support of the people who count, i.e., the educated class in and out of government service . . . not to mention the American people.[143]

Throughout the coup deliberations Administration officials continued to express anxiety about the outcome and ramifications. McGeorge Bundy, special assistant to Kennedy for national security affairs, was worried about the United States "reaping blame" for an unsuccessful effort; he was "particularly concerned about hazards that an unsuccessful coup, however carefully we avoid direct engagement, will be laid at our door by public opinion almost everywhere."[144] Despite the problems, the Administration went ahead with plans for the coup. Kennedy cabled Lodge on October 30, stating that the U.S. posture in the event of a coup was to

reject appeals for direct intervention from either side, and [U.S.] resources will not be committed between the battle lines or in support of either side, without authorization from Washington. . . .
    But once a coup under responsible leadership has begun . . . it is in the interest of the U.S. government that it should succeed.[145]

Diem called Lodge on the day of the coup and asked him about the "attitude of the U.S." Lodge, who had been in favor of it from the start, told Diem:

I do not feel well enough informed to be able to tell you. . . . You have certainly done your duty. . . . I admire your courage and great contributions to your country. No one can take away from you the credit for all you have done. Now I am worried about your physical safety. . . . If I can do anything for your physical safety, please call me.[146]

The Pentagon Papers report that the "brutal . . . pointless murder of Diem and Nhu . . . was received in Washington with shock and dismay." Kennedy was "reportedly . . . stunned" by the news, for apparently the United States had put "full confidence in the coup committee's offers of safe conduct to the brothers and . . . we had not appreciated the degree of hatred of the Ngo family among the generals." The South Vietnamese reaction to the killings was said to be one of "popular jubilation," including "[s]pontaneous street demonstrations by students," which ended in the burning of the *Times of Vietnam* office in Saigon. "Americans were greeted and received with great enthusiasm. . . . Vietnamese were heard to remark that if an election for president were held, Lodge would win by a landslide."[147]

Immediate U.S. concern was how to react to the coup in terms of official public posture. Secretary Rusk felt that the United States had to delay recognizing the new government so that the officials would not appear to be "U.S. agents or stooges"; this would assist the official U.S. "public stance of noncomplicity." He also "discouraged" any large group of generals from seeing Lodge, lest people think they were "'reporting in.'" A message from Rusk to Lodge "stressed the need to underscore publically the fact that this was not so much a coup as an expression of national will."[148]

The first act of the new "Revolutionary Committee" was the distribution of leaflets and press releases announcing the "dissolution of the National Assembly and the abolition of the Diem-Nhu government . . . and proclaiming the support . . . for such democratic principles as free elections, unhampered political opposition, freedom of the press, freedom of religion, and end to discrimination."[149] The new regime included six generals among fifteen cabinet members. *The Pentagon Papers* indicate that political leaders "were conspicuously absent" from the group, "a fact which would impair the new government's securing . . . popular support."[150]

CONCLUSION

As difficult as it is to summarize this nine-year period in the Vietnamese struggle for national liberation, some things are clear. The Pentagon historians contend that "[it] was a situation without good alternatives." While the Diem regime offered some "stability and authority, its repressive actions against the Buddhists had permanently alienated popular support with a high probability of victory for the Viet Cong." This support placed the United States in a "weak and manipulable position on important internal issues." Having "no 'alternatives'" to Diem greatly limited our influence over the regime and ruled out the kinds of power Washington might have employed. "Aware of our fundamental commitment to him, Diem could with relative impunity ignore our wishes."[151] The Pentagon authors further contend that neither Kennedy nor any other President could do any less in the situation than he did; they felt that the choices were the only choices then and assert that years later they remain the only choices he could have made.[152]

While the Pentagon historians argue that the situation in Vietnam was without good alternatives, the only real choice for the Vietnamese people was the liberation struggle led by the NLF, to free Vietnam from all foreign invaders and regimes set up by those invaders. However, since *The Pentagon Papers* begin with a basic support for the guiding premises and objectives of American policy, this alternative is outside their definition of the situation.

Carl Oglesby, author of a book on Vietnam and a former spokesman for the antiwar movement in the United States, has placed these guiding premises and objectives of American policy (the Free World, democracy, the domino theory) in an economic and political context which suggests that the real reasons for U.S. involvement in Vietnam were imperialism and counterrevolution. Oglesby argues that the "issue of the Vietnam war is not Western freedom versus Eastern slavery but foreign versus local control of Vietnam. . . . The war is being fought to determine how and by whom the Vietnamese political economy is going to be developed." He cites a 1938 U.S. Naval Intelligence report to support his analysis: *"Realistically, all wars have been fought for economic reasons. To make them politically and socially palatable, ideological issues have always been invoked. Any possible future war will, undoubtedly, conform to historical precedent."*[153]

Richard DuBoff, co-author of *America's Vietnam Policy: The Strategy of Deception*, has examined National Security Council documents from 1949 to 1954, a crucial time in the French-Vietnamese struggle. He supports Oglesby's analysis by pointing to four major themes that emerged from U.S. policy during this period, all aimed at maintaining American imperialism in the Southeast Asian-Pacific region. These themes remained intact during the Diem years.

1. Southeast Asia was viewed as an essential part of a Pacific rimlands political economy. . . .
2. Were any part to "fall" or opt out of the free [enterprise] world, the repercussions would be felt throughout the area, particularly in Japan. . . .
3. "Loss" of Indochina would have further grave domino effects . . . on America's power as guarantor of "order" and "stability."
4. No negotiations whatever were to be considered with Communists over the future of Southeast Asia.[154]

Much was made of the "domino theory" during the Diem years. Gabriel Kolko, historian and author of numerous works on American foreign policy, calls this theory a "counterrevolutionary doctrine which defined modern history as a movement of Third World and dependent nations . . . away from the colonialism of capitalism and toward national revolution and forms of socialism." One cannot "divorce the economic and strategic components of the so-called domino theory. . . . To confront this synthesis of concerns is to comprehend the truly imperialist nature of American policy in Southeast Asia." The Diem regime was not the main issue, but rather "the future of Southeast Asia and, beyond it, the relation of Vietnam to revolution in modern times."[155]

Eqbal Ahmad argues that Vietnam is a "unique case," and that it cannot be placed within the context of the domino theory.

Vietnam is the only country . . . where the nationalist movement for independence was led by the Communists during its most crucial and heroic decades. . . . Ho Chi Minh and his associates . . . are understandably considered the founding fathers of modern Vietnam. It was morbid optimism to expect an absentee aristocrat to supplant a leader who had devoted a lifetime to the liberation of his country, and to defeat a leadership and cadres whose organic ties with the peasants were cemented by the bitter struggle for independence.[156]

The truth of the matter is that the United States, in violation of international agreements and solemn promises, created and sustained an oppressive regime against the increasing political opposition of its own people. Such policies were a continuation of French and Japanese colonialism and they spawned a popular resistance movement, led by the Viet Minh and the National Liberation Front. This nationalist struggle would expand in the post-Diem period and be confronted by a growing American military force, as the Vietnam War entered yet another historic phase, that of escalation and Vietnamization.

NOTES

1. George McTurnan and John W. Lewis, *The United States in Vietnam* (New York: Dial Press, 1967), p. 66.

2. Robert Scheer and Warren Hinkle, "The 'Vietnam Lobby,'" in *Ramparts Vietnam Primer* (San Francisco: Ramparts Press, 1966), pp. 24–25.

3. The Senator Gravel Edition, *The Pentagon Papers: The Defense Department History of United States Decisionmaking on Vietnam*, 5 vols. (Boston: Beacon Press, 1972), I: 299. This is the Gravel Edition of *The Pentagon Papers* and hereafter will be cited as GE.

4. Jean Lacouture, *Vietnam: Between Two Truces* (New York: Random House, 1966), p. 79.

5. *The Pentagon Papers*, GE I, 299.

6. Cited in Charles Haynie and John Heckman, *The Rebellion Against the Diem Regime, 1957-58* (Ithaca, N.Y.: Cornell Ad-Hoc Committee to End the War in Vietnam, 1965), pp. 10-11.

7. *The Pentagon Papers*, GE I, 220, 230-34; Haynie and Heckman, p. 6.

8. Bernard Fall, *The Two Viet-Nams* (New York: Praeger, 1963), p. 257.

9. Ibid.

10. Ibid.

11. U.S. Cong., Senate, *Background Information Related to Southeast Asia and Vietnam*, 89th Cong., 1st sess. (Washington, D.C.: GPO, 1965), p. 71.

12. Cited in Haynie and Heckman, pp. 11-12.

13. *The Pentagon Papers*, GE I, 211.

14. U.S. Cong., House, *United States-Vietnam Relations, 1945-1967: Study Prepared by the Department of Defense*, 12 vols. (Washington, D.C.: GPO, 1971), 10:274-75. This is the U.S. Government edition of *The Pentagon Papers* and hereafter will be cited as USG ed.

15. Ibid., p. 737.

16. Quoted in Ibid., 574.

17. Wilfred Burchett, "The Receiving End," in *The Pentagon Papers: Critical Essays*, eds. Noam Chomsky and Howard Zinn, GE V, p. 63.

18. Nina Adams, "The Last Line of Defense," *The Pentagon Papers: Critical Essays*, eds. Noam Chomsky and Howard Zinn, GE V, 152.

19. Quoted in Chomsky, *For Reasons of State* (New York: Random House, 1973), p. 100.

20. *The Pentagon Papers*, GE I, 211, 213.

21. Chomsky, p. 101.

22. Quoted in *Background Information*, p. 85.

23. Quoted in Noam Chomsky and Edward S. Herman, *Counter-Revolutionary Violence: Bloodbaths in Fact and Propaganda* (Andover, Mass.: Warner Modular Publications, 1973), p. 17.

24. Joseph Buttinger, *Vietnam: A Dragon Embattled*, 2 vols. (New York: Praeger, 1967), 2:976.

25. Jeffrey Race, *War Comes to Long An* (Berkeley: University of California Press, 1972), pp. 37, 40.

26. Ibid., p. 67.

27. Buttinger, p. 977.

28. Robert Scheer, *How the United States Got Involved in Vietnam* (Santa Barbara: The Fund for the Republic, 1965), pp. 34-36.

29. *The Pentagon Papers*, GE I, 255.

30. Cited in Haynie and Heckman, p. 13.

31. Nguyen Kien, *Le Sud Vietnam Depuis Dien-bien-phu* (Paris: 1963), p. 66, cited in Ibid., p. 14.

32. Quoted in Ibid., p. 11.

33. David Hotham, "General Considerations of American Programs," in *Vietnam: The First Five Years*, ed. Richard Lindholm (East Lansing: Michigan State University Press, 1959), p. 347.

34. *The Pentagon Papers*, GE I, 256.

35. Ibid., p. 257.

36. Quoted in Haynie and Heckman, p. 28.

37. Quoted in *The Pentagon Papers*, GE I, 252.

38. Ibid.

39. Joseph Kraft, Introduction to Jean Lacouture, *Vietnam: Between Two Truces* (New York: Random House, 1966), p. xii, xiii.

40. Race, p. 71.

41. *The Pentagon Papers*, GE I, 248.

42. Lacouture, p. 24.

43. Quoted in *Background Information*, p. 67.

44. Quoted in Robert Scheer, "Hang Down Your Head Tom Dooley," in *Ramparts Vietnam Primer* (San Francisco: Ramparts Press, 1966), p. 16.

45. Quoted in Ibid., p. 19.

46. Fall, *The Two Viet-Nams*, p. 257.

47. Scheer, pp. 14–21.

48. Chomsky, "The Pentagon Papers as Propaganda and History," *The Pentagon Papers: Critical Essays*, eds. Noam Chomsky and Howard Zinn, GE V, 188.

49. Quoted in *Vietnam: History, Documents, and Opinions on a World Crisis*, ed. Marvin Gettleman (Greenwich, Conn.: Fawcett, 1965), p. 164.

50. Ibid.

51. *The Pentagon Papers*, USG ed., 10, 274.

52. *The Pentagon papers*, GE I, 177.

53. Quoted in Chomsky, *For Reasons of State*, p. 104.

54. Quoted in *Background Information*, p. 72.

55. Ibid.

56. Scheer and Hinkle, p. 32.

57. *The Pentagon Papers*, GE I, 239.

58. Quoted in Haynie and Heckman, p. 8.

59. Lacouture, pp. 28–29.

60. *The Pentagon Papers*, GE I, 239, 245.

61. George McTurnan Kahin, Address to the InterFaith Seminar for Clergy on Vietnam, Boston University, October 1, 1965, p. 3.

62. *The Pentagon Papers*, GE I, 310.

63. Quoted in Race, p. 67.

64. Ibid., p. 89.

65. Scheer, p. 21.

66. Ibid., p. 28.

67. Robert Scigliano, *South Vietnam: Nation Under Stress* (Boston: Houghton Mifflin, 1964), pp. 121-23.

68. *The Pentagon Papers*, GE I, 254-55.

69. Quoted in Ibid., II, 148.

70. Ibid., 130.

71. Ibid., 133.

72. Bernard Fall, *Street Without Joy* (London: Pall Mall, 1964), p. 346.

73. Quoted in Edward S. Herman and Richard DuBoff, *How to Coo Like a Dove While Fighting to Win: The Public Relations of the Johnson Policy in Vietnam*, 2nd ed., rev. (New York: Clergy and Laymen Concerned About Vietnam, 1969), p. 7.

74. Dallas *Morning News*, January 1, 1963.

75. *The Pentagon Papers*, GE II, 149.

76. Quoted in Ibid., 149.

77. Ibid., p. 159.

78. Chomsky, "The Pentagon Papers as Propaganda and History," p. 183.

79. Quoted in *Background Information*, p. 82.

80. Quoted in *The Pentagon Papers*, GE II, 98-99.

81. Ibid., 63.

82. Ibid., I, 259.

83. Ibid., 265.

84. Chomsky, "The Pentagon Papers as Propaganda and History," p. 185.

85. Quoted in Ibid.

86. *The Pentagon Papers*, GE I, 260.

87. Lacouture, p. 176.

88. Ibid., pp. 53-55.

89. Quoted in Ibid., pp. 58-59.

90. Eqbal Ahmad, "Revolutionary Warfare: How to Tell When the Rebels Have Won," *The Nation* 201 (August 30, 1965): 96-99.

91. Ibid., p. 98.

92. Fall, *The Two Viet-Nams*, p. 344.

93. Fall, *Street Without Joy*, p. 373.

94. Ahmad, p. 98.

95. Bernard Fall, *Last Reflections on a War* (New York: Doubleday, 1967), pp. 233–34.

96. Susan Brownmiller, *Against Our Will: Men, Women and Rape* (New York: Bantam, 1975), p. 92.

97. Herman and DuBoff, p. 36.

98. Haynie and Heckman, p. 5.

99. *The Pentagon Papers*, GE I, 225.

100. Haynie and Heckman, p. 21.

101. Kahin, pp. 3–4.

102. Quoted in *The Pentagon Papers*, GE I, 288.

103. Scheer and Hinkle, pp. 31–32.

104. Quoted in James Aronson, "The Media and the Message," *The Pentagon Papers: Critical Essays*, eds. Noam Chomsky and Howard Zinn, GE V, 49.

105. Quoted in *Background Information*, p. 73.

106. Cited in Scheer and Hinkle, p. 24.

107. Ibid.

108. Quoted in *The Pentagon Papers*, GE I, 298.

109. Ibid., 266.

110. Ibid., 267.

111. Quoted in Ibid., II, 95.

112. Quoted in *Background Information*, p. 84.

113. Quoted in *The Pentagon Papers*, GE II, 105–6.

114. Ibid., 90–91.

115. Ibid., 93.

116. Ibid., 88.

117. Ibid., 656.

118. Ibid., 657.

119. Noam Chomsky, personal communication, May 1976.

120. *The Pentagon Papers*, GE II, 657.

121. Ibid., 173.

122. Ibid., 174.

123. Ibid., 164.

124. Lacouture, p. 76.

125. *The Pentagon Papers,* GE II, 226.

126. Ibid., 226–27.

127. Ibid., 227.

128. Ibid., 227–28.

129. Ibid., 232.

130. Ibid., 236.

131. Quoted in Ibid., 235.

132. Ibid., 252.

133. Ibid., 202.

134. Ibid., 225.

135. Ibid., 231.

136. Ibid., 185.

137. Ibid., 241.

138. Quoted in Ibid., 241.

139. Ibid., 207.

140. Ibid., 250–51.

141. Quoted in Ibid., 253.

142. Quoted in Ibid., 251.

143. Quoted in Ibid., 239.

144. Quoted in Ibid., 259.

145. Quoted in Ibid., 263.

146. Quoted in Ibid., 268.

147. Ibid., 270.

148. Ibid.

149. Ibid., 271.

150. Ibid., 271–72.

151. Ibid., 201, 203.

152. Ibid., 103.

153. Carl Oglesby, "Vietnam Crucible: An Essay on the Meanings of the Cold War," in *Containment and Change,* Carl Oglesby and Richard Schaull (New York: Macmillan, 1967), pp. 112, 165.

154. Richard B. DuBoff, "Business Ideology and Foreign Policy," *The Pentagon Papers: Critical Essays,* eds. Noam Chomsky and Howard Zinn, GE V, 27.

155. Gabriel Kolko, "The American Goals in Vietnam," *The Pentagon Papers: Critical Essays,* eds. Noam Chomsky and Howard Zinn, GE V, 2, 14.

156. Ahmad, p. 99.

6

Escalation—Vietnamization—
End of the War

ESCALATION UNDER PRESIDENT JOHNSON

In late 1963 significant planning took place within the U.S. government that would begin to change the nature of the war. National Security Action Memorandum 273 (NSAM 273) became the cornerstone of America's policy in Vietnam in stating as our goal, "to assist the people and Government of that country [South Vietnam] to win their contest against the externally directed and supported Communist conspiracy." It directed that the level of both economic and military support be maintained at least as high as the support given to Diem and called for planning of covert action by South Vietnam against the North. In his first Vietnam policy statement, President Johnson ordered officials at the State Department to document a strong case "to demonstrate to the world the degree to which the Viet Cong is controlled, sustained and supplied from Hanoi, through Laos and other channels."[1]

In effecting this policy, the U.S., as revealed in *The Pentagon Papers*, had been carrying out secret military attacks against North Vietnam six months prior to the Gulf of Tonkin incident in August 1964. President Johnson ordered covert military operations against North Vietnam (Operation Plan 34A) on February 1, 1964. The plan included kidnappings of North Vietnamese citizens for intelligence purposes, V-2 spy flights over North Vietnam, commando raids to hit rail and highway bridges, the parachuting of psychological-warfare and sabotage teams into North Vietnam, and the shelling of the North's coastal installations by PT boats. Washington's secret war against North Vietnam also included air operations in Laos. Although the planes had Laotian markings, some of the planes were flown by Air America pilots, a CIA-operated airline.[2]

But as the Johnson Administration increased the intensity of the covert war, it simultaneously began planning for a conventional war against North Vietnam. The position had hardened in rejecting completely the possibility of immediate American withdrawal from Vietnam. The last voice raised in support of that policy alternative was Paul Kattenburg's, from the Vietnam Working Group. In the summer of 1963 he argued for withdrawal and concluded that "we are going to be thrown out of the country in six months."[3] However, as the escalation continued to increase, that appraisal was never even considered by the highest councils of U.S. war planners.

At the Honolulu Conference held on November 20, 1963, Ambassador Henry Cabot Lodge, in his negative assessment of the Vietnamese situation, urged the post-Diem government to take action "to consolidate its popular support." Specifically, Lodge urged "efforts to eliminate forced labor in the strategic hamlets, to curtail arbitrary arrests, to deal with extortion and corruption, to enlist the support of the Hoa Hao and Cao Dai sects, and to consolidate and strengthen the strategic hamlet program." However, Lodge argued that the new government should not be "press[ed] too much" to democratize and constitutionalize the country.[4]

December 1963 brought news from Long An province of the near collapse of the strategic hamlet program. The strategic hamlet program was a South Vietnamese-U.S. plan to relocate, many times forceably, South Vietnamese peasants in order to isolate them from the Viet Cong. This attempt to deny VC guerrillas contact with the rural population was bitterly resented by a peasantry forced to leave their ancestral homes (see page 140). The South Vietnamese Army (ARVN) was unable or unwilling to support villages under attack, and the hamlets were increasingly being captured by the Viet Cong. Secretary of Defense Robert McNamara's visit to South Vietnam in December of that year confirmed that the situation had deteriorated since the preceding summer. He recommended to President Johnson the strengthening of ARVN formations in the key provinces, increased American military and civilian staffs and the initiation of a new "pacification" program, and "a wide variety of sabotage and psychological operations against North Vietnam."[5]

On January 30, 1964, General Nguyen Khanh led an internal, bloodless coup that was successful in removing from power the short-lived General Duong Van Minh junta that followed the Diem coup. General Khanh justified the coup as necessary to counteract a growing neutralist movement. Johnson equated neutralization of South Vietnam with a Communist takeover and therefore Khanh's junta in Saigon received immediate U.S. support. However, the pacification program continued to falter, and Khanh's performance was criticized in a U.S. report that concluded: "In many of the most critical provinces, pacification programs remain at a virtual standstill and there is an evident lack of urgency and clear direction."[6]

Early in 1964 considerable concern was expressed on the part of top U.S. officials over growing neutralist sentiment in Saigon. William P. Bundy, Assistant Secretary of State for Far Eastern Affairs, called the neutralization approach the

"Vietnam solution" and said it must be prevented. On March 17, the U.S. position was made clear when McNamara declared: "We seek an independent, non-Communist South Vietnam."[7] In a cablegram to Ambassador Lodge in Saigon, dated March 20, 1964, President Johnson stated that he was intent on "knocking down the idea of neutralization wherever it rears its ugly head, and on this point I think nothing is more important than to stop neutralist talk wherever we can by whatever means we can."[8] Johnson's fear of the U.S. ability to control a coalition government in South Vietnam was becoming more obvious.

U.S. policy attention was shifting from treating only symptoms in South Vietnam to getting at the "cause" of the problem, which was Hanoi. Lodge urged the use of a "carrot and stick" approach to North Vietnam: The United States would offer Hanoi economic aid if they would stop supporting the Viet Cong. If North Vietnam refused the "carrot," the United States would begin previously threatened punitive strikes, but it would not admit to the attacks publicly.[9] Over the next few years the "stick" became the official U.S. policy. In contrast to this approach, the National Liberation Front had issued a manifesto on November 8, 1963, to the Military Revolutionary Council of General Duong Van Minh, calling on all concerned parties in South Vietnam to negotiate a cease-fire, solve the nation's problems and work toward free general elections in order to form a national coalition government representative of the South Vietnamese people.[10]

A group of American scholars issued a Citizens' White Paper, *The Politics of Escalation in Vietnam*, calling attention to the official projected myth of American commitment to a negotiated settlement. The authors state: "The most disturbing finding of this study is thus the pattern in which moves toward political settlement are brought to a close with an intensification of the war by the U.S."[11] They reveal that U.N. Secretary General U Thant, French President de Gaulle, and the Soviet Union all called for a Geneva

Conference to be held during the week of July 23, 1964. During the week of August 2, 1964, the United States made its first overt attacks on territory and ships of North Vietnam. Anti-American protests in cities of South Vietnam in January 1965 and attacks on U.S. airfields by the NLF were followed by U.S. bombing of North Vietnam on February 7, 1965. And in November and December 1965, the negotiation efforts of Italian intermediaries Professor Giorgio LaPira and Foreign Minister Amintore Fanfani, were followed by the first bombing of the Haiphong area (on December 15), "which the Administration had been told would close the door to negotiations."[12] The study closes: "One conclusion can be asserted unequivocally: The U.S. increased its commitment to a prolongation of the Vietnam war at a time when the drift of the Saigon junta and of public opinion was in the direction of negotiations for a neutralized Vietnam."[13]

Noam Chomsky summarizes the U.S. position on negotiations during this period:

The United States rejected any such "premature negotiations" [NLF attempts throughout 1964 to negotiate a "Laos settlement"—a neutralist coalition government] as incompatible with its goal of maintaining a non-Communist South Vietnam under American control. The reason was quite simple. As American officials constantly reiterated, the NLF was the only significant political force and the U.S.-imposed regime had virtually no popular base.[14]

Because the U.S. chose force over negotiations, they supported the efforts of General Khanh and South Vietnam's Armed Forces Council during this period. But Chomsky observes:

By January 1965, even that last hope went up in smoke. As Ambassador Taylor explained in his memoirs . . . the United States government "had lost confidence in Khanh" by late 1965. He lacked "character and integrity," added Taylor sadly. The clearest evidence of Khanh's lack of character was that by late January he was moving towards "a dangerous Khanh-Buddhist alliance which might eventually lead to an unfriendly government with which we could not work."[15]

As indicated in the Citizens' White Paper, the Soviet Union, France, and North Vietnam urged the 14 nations that had participated in the 1961-62 Geneva Conference on Laos to reconvene in the summer of 1964. Prompt, positive support came from China, Cambodia, and the NLF, but the Johnson Administration showed no willingness to explore this possibility for a peaceful settlement. Instead Johnson announced, "We do not believe in conferences called to ratify terror," and on the following day he increased the number of U.S. troops in South Vietnam from 16,000 to 21,000—a 30 percent increase.[16] Later in the year, U Thant again pleaded for negotiations between the United States and North Vietnam. He specifically proposed that Washington and Hanoi send emissaries to Rangoon, Burma, to negotiate. The North Vietnamese accepted, but Johnson refused to enter into discussions until after the November elections.

Even after Johnson's landslide victory, with Hanoi still willing to negotiate, the United States followed Defense Secretary McNamara, who "flatly opposed the attempt."[17] Not until March 9, 1965, when the New York *Times* reported U Thant's efforts at setting up peace negotiations and U.S. rejection of same, was the American public made aware of Johnson's unwillingness to negotiate. Robert McCloskey, State Department spokesman, "explained" that Secretary of State Rusk's "antennae is sensitive," and if Hanoi was "prepared for serious talks . . . the Secretary of State said he would recognize it when it came."[18]

Following the February 1965 Viet Cong raid on American barracks at Pleiku and the retaliatory U.S. bombing of North Vietnam,[19] U Thant, the Soviet Union, and France once again called for negotiations—to be held either inside or outside the United Nations—and for another attempt at the Geneva Conference. Clearly frustrated by the Johnson Administration's continued rejection of peace proposals, U Thant appealed directly to the American public. He stated:

"I am sure that the great American people, if they know the true facts and the background to the developments in South Vietnam, will agree with me that further bloodshed is unnecessary"; and he added, "in times of war and hostilities the first casualty is truth."[20] The Johnson Administration continued to insist on a permanent division of Vietnam and made it clear that the United States would not accept any settlement that did not recognize South Vietnam as a separate and sovereign entity.[21]

Washington's fixed notion on negotiation was further crystallized by William Bundy:

Negotiation will in the end certainly be an answer if it produces an independent and secure South Viet-Nam. But, on the other hand, there's no sign that Hanoi would really go for that at the present time. And negotiation that admitted communism to South Viet-Nam or legalized it, that did not get Hanoi and the North Vietnamese out, or that set up some structure under nebulous, not very clear guarantees, simply would not provide the independent and secure South Viet-Nam that nation is entitled to and that we're after.[22]

Although Bundy argued that Hanoi and the North Vietnamese should get out of South Vietnam, *The Pentagon Papers* reveal that there was no known evidence of any regular North Vietnamese units in South Vietnam until April 1965, two months after Bundy's statement.[23] The chronology of this period in *The Pentagon Papers* led Chomsky to conclude:

The record is clear, then, that when the United States undertook the February escalation, it knew of no regular North Vietnamese units in South Vietnam, and that five months later, while implementing the plan to deploy 85,000 troops, the Pentagon was still speculating about the possibility that there might be PAVN [People's Army of North Vietnam] forces in or near South Vietnam. In the light of these facts, the discussion of whether the U.S. was defending South Vietnam from an "armed attack" from the North—the official U.S. governmental position—is ludicrous.[24]

One major result of the covert military operations included in Operation Plan 34A, mentioned above, was the Gulf of Tonkin incident. After exhaustive investigation of this incident, Anthony Austin concludes:

. . . the illogic of this account [the official story] becomes overwhelming and one is compelled to agree with Fulbright when he says, "The fact is there was no attack at all."

What remains, then, is a picture of policy formulation in Washington in which the managers of the national security establishment did not provoke an attack on an American patrol, or retaliate knowing there was no attack, or manufacture intelligence intercepts out of whole cloth but, exploiting an unexpected opportunity, deliberately misled Congress and the American people on the nature of the patrol and the evidence of an attack and through that deception were able to obtain Congressional authorization for a war they had secretly decided on months before, while promising the voters peace.[25]

Walt Rostow, then counselor in the State Department, summed up the Johnson Administration's relief in now having a "Pearl Harbor" rallying incident to unify a critical public. Rostow, two days after the Gulf of Tonkin incident commented: "We don't know what happened, but it had the desired result."[26] On August 7, Johnson received congressional support for U.S. policy in Vietnam.[27]

Shortly thereafter, McNamara asked the Joint Chiefs of Staff for a list of actions that would put military pressure on the North Vietnamese. The list they provided was lengthy and included increased use of Plan 34A covert operations, continuation of the DeSoto patrols (code name for the covert U.S. destroyer patrols in the Gulf of Tonkin), and supersonic flights over Hanoi in order to break all the windows in the capital city.[28] The Administration increased its planning for the open, escalated war to come while rejecting all peace overtures short of surrender. On August 7, 1964, Congress passed the Gulf of Tonkin Resolution, giving President Johnson the power to use force in "protecting the security of

Southeast Asia." On August 10, General Maxwell Taylor, in a report to Johnson, cited the major objective of the U.S. mission: "Be prepared to implement contingency plans against North Vietnam with optimum readiness by January 1, 1965." Thereafter, January 1 was referred to as D-Day.[29]

A study group headed by William Bundy was to recommend longer-range Vietnam options that would move beyond the post-Tonkin "tit-for-tat" (Pentagon term) reprisal ad hoc strategies. The group's report recommended three options to the President. Option A included reprisal air strikes and the intensification of covert pressures on the North Vietnamese. Option B called for bombing the North "at a fairly rapid pace and without interruption" until all U.S. demands were met. This was referred to as "fast full squeeze." The United States would define the negotiating position "in a way which makes Communist acceptance unlikely" if the U.S. was pressed to negotiate "before a Communist agreement to comply." Option C included a graduated air war with possible use of ground troops, referred to as "progressive squeeze-and-talk."[30]

The fabrication issued by the American government was that the South Vietnamese insurgents were "externally directed and supported" by a "Communist conspiracy." The intelligence assessment in 1961 was that "80–90% of the estimated 17,000 VC had been locally recruited, and that there was little evidence that the VC relied on external supplies."[31] The 1964 intelligence analysis similarly reported that "the primary sources of Communist strength in South Vietnam are indigenous."[32] However, the "war of aggression" from the North continued to be the description advanced to the public.

The Pentagon Papers revealed the truth, however. The United States was deploying troops *before* North Vietnamese troops appeared in South Vietnam. It is clear that U.S. ground forces were in combat in South Vietnam on March 8, 1965, while the first reference to regular North Vietnamese units was April 21, 1965.[33] And while the United States approved the deployment of American Marines in February 1965, in the summer of 1965 the Pentagon was still speculating about the *possibility* of North Vietnamese troops in South Vietnam. On July 1, 1965, planned U.S. deployments totaled 85,000 troops.[34] By mid-July the President had approved an increase in U.S. troop level to 175,000 in 1965, with an additional 100,000 increase for 1966.[35]

Toward the end of 1964 and into 1965, the decision-makers started to move from covert to overt warfare, and the escalation progressed.[36] The American war planners differed as to how the overt war should be carried out, but that the war should be escalated was nearly unanimous among the national security officials. However, only part of the escalation was in response to Viet Cong attacks on U.S. forces. Escalation was now planned to progressively hurt the enemy in order to meet the U.S. goal of defeating the communists in Vietnam. Overt and covert U.S. provocation *preceded* the Viet Cong attacks: of November 1, 1964, on Bien Hoa Airfield; of December 24, 1964, on a U.S. barracks in Saigon; and of a February 7, 1965, mortar attack on a U.S. installation in Pleiku.[37] U.S. military "advisers" had been leading ARVN troops in battle for years, and the U.S. had been bombing "free fire zones" since the early 1960s. The February attack led Johnson to order reprisal air attacks against the North.

The master bombing plan, "Rolling Thunder," grew out of the Sullivan Task Force, which Johnson had instituted in December 1963. The group included officials from the Department of Defense, the White House, the Air Force, the CIA, and the State Department. The Sullivan group urged caution or skepticism on the efficacy of bombing as a means of ending the war. They reported that North Vietnam was capable of taking much punishment before surrendering or accepting a settlement on U.S. terms. The report also warned that the U.S. would appear to be a "bully" and further tarnish its international image. With all these misgivings, the group rationalized the bombing move on the basis of "exploiting DRV concern over its loss of industry." The Sullivan group theorized that the North Vietnamese leadership was proud of their industrial gains and could be pressured by a U.S. bombing threat to destroy that industrial complex. On the crucial goal of bombing to force North Vietnam to stop the Viet Cong insurgency in South Vietnam, the Sullivan report stated it was "doubtful that Hanoi could call off the insurgency."[38] Ralph Stavins, et al., summarize the report:

> If the U.S. started the bombing, the North would be unable or unwilling to call off the insurgency: unable because the insurgency was Southern, unwilling because the North, once it was attacked by the United States, would, in fact, positively support the insurgency. . . . Rolling Thunder was viewed as escalating and irreversible. . . . The bombing campaign would result in an indefinite war, continuously escalating, with both sides embroiled in a perpetual stalemate.[39]

The authors also observe: "Conspicuously absent from these surveys was any study of American public opinion."[40] The nation and Congress were kept in the dark about the Administration's plan for escalation.

Congress had not been informed that the Administration had decided to go to war prior to Tonkin but had deferred the go-ahead signal until after the election. Congress was not advised of the extensive preparation for war, or appraised of the Administration's view that once it obtained a joint resolution, the light would shift from amber to green. Congress was simply told that the Executive needed the power to be flexible. . . . Congress was seduced into supporting the preordained decision of the Executive to wage an aggressive war against North Vietnam. . . . In sum, the Executive deceived the Congress into believing that the Administration had done nothing to incur the attack and that the resolution might or might not be employed in the future.[41]

From November 1963 to the end of 1964 the war was characterized by increasing American involvement: first, in the form of provocative programs such as the covert destroyer DeSoto patrols, which eventually led to the Gulf of Tonkin incident, and second, in the Administration's decision to carry out air strikes against the North. These strikes were represented as retaliatory, although *The Pentagon Papers* document the careful planning to put direct military pressure on "the enemy" and the disinclination to negotiate or allow a neutralist position to materialize in South Vietnam.

Senate Foreign Relations Chairman J. William Fulbright openly regretted the role he, his committee and the overwhelming number of the Congress played in the aftermath of the Tonkin Gulf incident. Fulbright wrote:

Congress was asked to show its support for the President in a crisis . . . without question or hesitation, it did so. The Senate Foreign Relations and Armed Services Committees endorsed the resolution [Tonkin Gulf Resolution] after perfunctory hearings and with only one dissenting vote on the morning of August 6.

Since its adoption the Administration has converted the Vietnamese conflict from a civil war in which some American advisors were involved to a major international war in which the principal fighting unit is an American army of hundreds of thousands of men. Each time Senators have raised questions about successive escalations of the war, we have the blank check of August 7, 1964, waved in our faces as supposed evidence of the overwhelming support of the Congress for a policy in Southeast Asia which in fact has been radically changed since the summer of 1964.

Had we met our responsibility of careful examination of a Presidential request, had the Senate Foreign Relations Committee held hearings on the resolution before recommending its adoption, had the Senate debated the resolution and considered its implications before giving its overwhelming approval, and specifically had we investigated carefully and thoroughly the alleged unprovoked attacks on our ships, we might have put limits and qualifications on our endorsement of future uses of force in Southeast Asia, if not in the resolution itself then in the legislative history preceding its adoption. As it was, only Senators [Wayne] Morse of Oregon and [Ernest] Gruening of Alaska opposed the resolution.[42]

The year 1965 is frequently marked as the starting point of the escalation that would peak in 1968 and see the introduction of more than a half million U.S. troops in South Vietnam. As cited above, it was in February, 1965, that President Johnson ordered air attacks on North Vietnam in retaliation for guerrilla raids in South Vietnam that had killed several Americans. On March 2, 1965, Johnson ordered the first nonretaliatory bombing raids on North Vietnam, and on March 6, he sent two U.S. Marine battalions to Danang, South Vietnam. On March 9, the President lifted the restriction on the use of napalm in strikes on the North.[43]

Even more devastating was the escalation of the bombing in South Vietnam. While President Johnson was ordering air strikes in North Vietnam in February 1965, "for the first time, U.S. jet aircraft were authorized to support the South Vietnamese Air Force in ground operations in the South without restriction."[44] By 1966 the bombing of the South had become three times greater than the intensity of the bombing of the North.[45] Of this 1965 U.S. policy Bernard Fall observed: "What changed the character of the Vietnam war was *not* the decision to bomb North Vietnam; *not* the decision to use American ground troops in South Vietnam; but the decision to wage unlimited aerial warfare inside the country at the price of literally pounding the place to bits."[46]

In early March 1965 the Administration began to abandon the retaliatory rationale for the bombing and emphasized the action "as part of a 'continuing' effort to resist aggression."[47] U.S. officials emphasized the war as one of foreign aggression, rejecting the explanation that is was, or had been, a civil war. Contradicting numerous previous statements by high-ranking government officials about the indigenous nature of the struggle in South Vietnam, Secretary Rusk stated: "I continue to hear and see nonsense about the nature of the struggle there. . . . There is no evidence that the Viet Cong has any significant popular following in South Vietnam."[48] In contrast, Eqbal Ahmad states: "In Vietnam, the signs are clear. The South Vietnamese regime has no legitimacy, and no government backed by a Western power can hope for popular support in a country where the Communists have capitalized on the nationalist appeal of restoring independence and unity, and where the pro-Western leaders have been Bao Dai, Diem, and the musical-chair generals."[49]

The American government's case of the "North as aggressor" was released on February 27, 1965, in a 64-page White Paper which demonstrated that "above all the war in Vietnam is *not* a spontaneous and local rebellion against the established government. . . . In Vietnam a Communist government has set out deliberately to conquer a sovereign people in a neighboring state." The report claimed "massive evidence of North Vietnamese aggression."[50] Later, however, a State Department official admitted the White Paper was an embarrassment and complimented independent journalist I. F. Stone for exposing the fact that only 2.5 percent of the total weapons captured by the United States between June 1962 and January 1964 (197 out of 7,555) were of North Vietnamese, Czech, Chinese, or Soviet manufacture.[51]

In April 1965 President Johnson proclaimed China to be the enemy force behind the North Vietnamese "aggressors":

Over this war—all Asia—is another reality: the deepening shadow of Communist China. The rulers in Hanoi are urged on by Peiping. . . . It is a nation which is helping the forces of violence in almost every continent. The contest in Vietnam is part of a wider pattern of aggressive purposes.[52]

The People's Republic of China took the position that the United States should completely and immediately withdraw from South Vietnam. This was a more extreme position than the Soviet Union's, and it tended to widen further the Sino-Soviet split.

International pressures for negotiations repeated the pleas that followed the 1964 American escalations. France and the

Soviet Union, as well as U Thant and Pope Paul, proposed plans to move from the battlefield to the negotiating table. In mid-March seventeen nonaligned nations issued a plea to all parties for immediate negotiations "without posing any preconditions."[53] On April 2, Canadian Prime Minister Lester Pearson suggested a bombing pause in order to encourage negotiations, but the Johnson Administration refused.[54] In a speech at Johns Hopkins University on April 7, President Johnson recognized the seventeen-nation appeal but made no mention of negotiations without preconditions.[55] The critics of his speech noted that the use of the ambiguous term "discussions" in place of "negotiations" was a sign of unwillingness to negotiate with Hanoi.[56] Instead, in what *The Pentagon Papers* refer to as "the Billion Dollar Carrot," Johnson promised a billion-dollar investment in Southeast Asia once peace was restored.[57]

A key document revealing how the U.S. policy on Vietnam was being escalated is NSAM 328 (April 6, 1965). In it McGeorge Bundy, special assistant to Presidents Kennedy and Johnson for National Security Affairs, 1961–66, reported Presidential decisions to the secretaries of State and Defense and the director of the CIA. Among the actions approved by the President: an 18–20,000-man increase in U.S. military support for South Vietnam; a major shift in the tactical mission of U.S. Marines from defensive to offensive missions; the use of Korean, Australian, and New Zealand troops to join U.S. Marines; continuation of the "Rolling Thunder" bombing plan; and the possibility of blockading or aerial mining of North Vietnam ports. Finally, in keeping with a policy of covert actions against both the "enemy" and mounting criticism at home, Johnson decreed that regarding the deployment of additional troops "premature publicity [should] be avoided by all possible precautions. The actions themselves should be taken as rapidly as practicable, but in ways that should minimize any appearance of sudden changes in policy."[58]

As the war intensified in 1965, the U.S. troop commitment rose from 23,000 to more than 180,000 by the end of the year.[59] The reports from Vietnam continued to conflict. From Secretary Dean Rusk: "Well, the South Korean personnel that are going into South Vietnam are not going there for combat purposes. They will be primarily engaged, I understand, on engineering tasks here and there." From a Senate hearing: *"Senator Gore:* 'Will you tell us what aid other countries are providing in Vietnam, if any.' *Mr. Bell,* former administrator, A.I.D.: 'Yes, sir. Fortunately we are not doing all the fighting. . . . There is a Korean division which is fighting there.' "[60]

The major statement from North Vietnam and the National Liberation Front during 1965 was Premier Pham Van Dong's four-point proposal for a settlement. It was issued on April 8 and endorsed by the NLF in September. Briefly, the four points called for a withdrawal of the United States from Vietnam, respect for the military provisions of the Geneva Agreements pending reunification of Vietnam, the South Vietnamese settling their own internal affairs according to the NLF's program, and the exclusion of foreign interference in the reunification of Vietnam.[61] It is important to note that the first point did *not* insist on withdrawal prior to negotiations, but only on agreement in principle to a late withdrawal.

Central to the negotiations problem was the issue of preconditions. Kahin and Lewis write:

At the beginning of the pause [the mid-May bombing pause] Secretary Dean Rusk secretly sent Hanoi a message, which it interpreted as an ultimatum demanding that the Vietcong lay down its arms as the price for a permanent cessation of American bombing of the North. Since the Rusk message and prompt resumption of the bombings so soon after its delivery confirmed Hanoi's mistrust of Washington's intentions with regard to negotiations, it is of great importance in understanding all subsequent responses from the Hanoi government to U.S. peace overtures. An awareness of the content of this message is also of importance in dispelling confusion concerning U.S. policies. *Not until Hanoi Radio broadcast Rusk's message on December 10, 1965, did a few American newspapers publish it and the American public learn what the Hanoi government had known for the previous six months* [emphasis added]. (Washington acknowledged the veracity of the report but stated it had no plans for releasing the text of the message.)[62]

Sections of the message the U.S. government concealed from the public conciliatory gestures include:

The highest authority in this government has asked me to inform Hanoi that there will be no air attacks on North Vietnam for a period beginning at noon, Washington time, Wednesday the 12th of May, and running into next week.

In taking this action, the United States is well aware of the risk that a temporary suspension of these air attacks may be understood as an indication of weakness, and it is therefore necessary for me to point out that if this pause should be misunderstood to demonstrate more clearly than ever, after the pause has ended, that the United States is determined not to accept aggression without reply in Vietnam.

Moreover, the United States must point out that the decision to end air attacks for this limited trial period is one which it must be free to reverse, if at any time in coming days, there should be actions by the other side in Vietnam which required immediate reply.[63]

Within the five days of the bombing pause, Hanoi was expected to meet with the National Liberation Front and to demonstrate to the United States "significant reductions" in armed actions that could be observed and reported by intelligence sources. Rusk's statement made no reference to negotiations and neglected to respond to Hanoi's earlier four points. However, the North Vietnamese did make a response as a result of the bombing pause. On May 18, a North Vietnamese diplomatic official, working through the French Foreign Office, indicated to the United States that if Premier Van Dong's four points (including U.S. withdrawal and self-determination for South Vietnam) "were accepted in principle, the application of the principle might be delayed over a very long time."[64]

For seven months the Johnson Administration denied the North Vietnamese move toward negotiations. In a speech on July 13, 1965, President Johnson told the American public: "I must say that candor compels me to tell you that there has not been the slightest indication that the other side is interested in negotiation or in unconditional discussions, although the United States has made some dozen separate attempts to bring that about."[65]

Speaking on July 28, 1965, the President again put on a restricting precondition when he offered unconditional discussions to "any government." Since the U.S. had consistently refused to recognize the National Liberation Front as a legitimate government, negotiations with the Viet Cong were ruled out. For the first time, at a postspeech press conference, Johnson, in an attempt to appear to support negotiations, said that in negotiations the Viet Cong "would have no difficulty being represented and having their views represented."[66] In the months that followed, considerable differences of interpretation between the NLF and the U.S. arose. The differences were cleared up, however, when on December 7 Dean Rusk stated that the United States would not compromise by granting any political status or influence to the National Liberation Front in South Vietnam.[67] The New York *Times* summarized his statements in an editorial: "The Secretary of State, while continuing to express readiness for negotiations on American terms, gives the impression of placing more faith in military measures than in diplomacy. He has virtually ruled out compromise with the Communists in South Vietnam. Hanoi either leaves South Vietnam alone or does not is a phrase that implies unconditional surrender rather than the unconditional negotiations President Johnson has been urging."[68]

In mid-December, while Italian Foreign Minister Amintore Fanfani was attempting to confirm a peace feeler from Hanoi that they were prepared to enter into negotiations *without* first requiring U.S. withdrawal, the United States launched its first air strike at a major industrial target in the Hanoi-Haiphong area.[69] The next day, December 16, Defense Secretary McNamara announced that the United States would continue such attacks. The damage to peace talks at this time was irreparable. The bombing pause between December 24, 1965, and January 31, 1966, was unproductive, and North Vietnam continued to criticize the United States for their lack of respect for the South Vietnamese peoples' right to self-determination.[70]

The bombing of North Vietnam had been systematic since March 2, 1965, and U.S. Government figures disclosed that by the end of 1965 more than 700,000 people (5 percent of the population) had been made refugees, and by mid-1966 the numbers exceeded one million. During 1965 the United States dropped more than one ton of bombs, napalm, and rockets for each of the Viet Cong reported to be fighting in South Vietnam. The ratio of civilian to Viet Cong casualties was reported to have run as high as 2 to 1.[71] The catalog of war horrors was rapidly multiplying. The abandoned farms caused food shortages, which increased South Vietnam's reliance on American aid; their economy weakened even further, and instability continued to plague South Vietnam's government.

On June 19, 1965, a military junta headed by Air Vice-Marshal Nguyen Cao Ky deposed Dr. Phan Huy Quat as Premier of South Vietnam. Quat's cabinet was alleged to be soft on Communism, and conservative elements (particularly the Catholics) feared, along with President Johnson, a neutralist settlement to the war, which would mean the establishment of a coalition government. Ky's cabinet was subordinated to the military National Leadership Committee, which was led by General Nguyen Van Thieu, a former defense minister who was instrumental in Quat's overthrow. Ky, announcing he would use the death penalty against hostile or corrupt elements in South Vietnam, issued a declaration of war for South Vietnam. He took a hard line on neutralists and embarrassed American officials by declaring that South Vietnam "needed a leadership like Adolf Hitler's." He later clarified the statement: "I want to infuse in our youth . . . the same dedication, the same fighting spirit as Hitler has infused in his people."[72]

The South Vietnam national election in September 1967 changed the Saigon regime leadership once again. Frances FitzGerald, in her prize-winning work on Vietnam, *Fire in the Lake*, states that up to the time of the election the United States had been supporting Ky as head of the regime, and "until it ceased to do so, there would be no chance for a civilian to win."[73] Ky took advantage of this support: He clamped down on newspaper censorship, limited the election campaign to one month (thus "granting himself the exclusive right to press his suit for all the intervening months"), and announced that he would overthrow anyone who won the election if he did not approve of his policies, explaining, "In any democratic country you have the right to disagree with the views of others."[74]

When all seemed set for a smooth Ky victory, General Thieu announced that he too would be a presidential candidate; the ruling generals were reportedly "shocked." A major conflict was averted, however, when after a tense three-day meeting of the ruling group, Ky announced that he would step down and run as vice-president on the Thieu ticket.[75]

The Thieu-Ky ticket won as expected, but with only 35 percent of the votes. Their strongest support came from "isolated military districts, where local commanders kept close watch over the voting." In the more politically sophisticated and less military controlled urban districts, the generals made such a poor showing that at the end of the day "their managers . . . stuffed ballot boxes with thousands of extra votes." The only surprise was that an unknown civilian named Truong Dinh Dzu, who, during the campaign, announced that he would recognize the NLF and support peace negotiations, came in second.[76]

The outcome of the election was predictable to those who

had followed recent South Vietnam history. Frances Fitz-
Gerald states that the election "ended up as a fiasco of noble
proportions."[78] And Robert Shaplen, correspondent in
Vietnam for *The New Yorker,* concludes:

> The assumption, primarily an American one, that the vote would
> have any salutary effect on the war, or on the internal political
> situation, was regarded by most Vietnamese as unwarranted and
> unrealistic. . . . Part of this reaction could be attributed to national
> cynicism, but much more was due to the conviction that the whole
> elective process had simply been an American-directed perform-
> ance with a Vietnamese cast.[79]

After the election the Thieu-Ky regime had a number of
the defeated candidates imprisoned, including Dzu, who was
given a five-year sentence. Although this was protested by
the AFL-CIO and civil liberties groups in the United States,
the State Department responded that "it had no control over
General Thieu's actions."[77] The election of the Thieu-Ky
regime had little affect on the Buddhist-nationalists and
their differences with the Saigon military government.

United States policy-makers throughout the war por-
trayed the struggle in terms of the Free World (Thieu and Ky)
against the Communist forces. The views of the Buddhists in
Vietnam and of others opposed to foreign domination,
known as the "third force," were consistently neglected, and
their viewpoints were either oversimplified or distorted by
the U.S. Government and much of the mass media. According to Kahin and Lewis:

> This arises in part as a consequence of Saigon's penchant for
> branding all political criticism as subversive. Because of this,
> Buddhist leaders who wish to remain politically active are obliged
> to obfuscate and camouflage their views in public to an extent that
> is confusing to outsiders.[80]

Tran Van Dinh, a former member of the South Vietnamese cabinet, summed up the basic aims of the Buddhists:
"Defense of Buddhism, anti-Communism, independence,

peace and social revolution through revival of authentic Vietnamese values and the reestablishment of national dignity."[81] Most Buddhist-nationalists viewed the war as ultimately destructive of their society and repeatedly called for political means to replace the futile military "solutions." They argued that a halting of the air and ground war in South Vietnam would open the way for a religious coalition, including the Catholics, to move toward a peaceful settlement.

THE TET OFFENSIVE

Frances FitzGerald quotes Robert Komer, director of pacification efforts in South Vietnam, just one week prior to Tet (the Vietnamese Lunar New Year): "We begin '68 in a better position than we have ever been before, but we've still got problems of bureaucratic inefficiency. There are still leadership difficulties that will degrade performance." However, she argues that the Tet Offensive "came as an almost total surprise to the Allied military command," when on January 31, 1968, NLF forces attacked almost every major American base (and every town and city in South Vietnam), including the large air base at Tan Son Nhut near Saigon, while a number of others entered Saigon itself. Liberation forces moved into the "'most secure' of the provincial capitals," and in many places they opened the jails and liberated Thieu's political prisoners. In Hué they occupied the university, the central marketplace, the imperial citadel, and the provincial headquarters.[82]

In Saigon the battle lasted nearly two weeks as NLF forces faced massive U.S. and ARVN ground and air attacks, which razed whole sections of the city and left thousands homeless. U.S. and ARVN forces also destroyed parts of Kontum City, Can Tho, Vinh Long, My Tho, and Ben Tre. (Ben Tre is the city about which one American adviser said, "We had to destroy it in order to save it.") After the fighting the American command estimated civilian dead at 165,000 during the fighting, with about 2 million new refugees.[83]

The Tet Offensive had a strong impact upon American public opinion, and "for the first time," FitzGerald reports, major news magazines began to "criticize the war overtly."[84] The "shock" of Tet was increased in the United States because Komer and Ambassador Ellsworth Bunker, who had replaced Henry Cabot Lodge, had been telling the people that "the enemy threat had receded. . . . The Americans had seemed to be firmly in control. . . . The fact that the American command had been unprepared for such a gross movement raised doubts about the quality of American intelligence and wisdom of American military strategy over the past two years." Nevertheless, one year later General William Westmoreland "claimed he had anticipated a major enemy offensive against the population areas around the time of Tet, and that he had prepared for it."[85]

FitzGerald states that Bunker and Westmoreland kept up a steady "facade of optimism, never expressing regret for the damages the Americans had wrought or fear for the political consequences." Bunker said that the Saigon army had "'demonstrated their ability' in fighting the Communists and 'gained confidence in themselves. . . . I think the people have gained confidence in them.'" Westmoreland was to write some months later: "The *Tet* offensive had the effect of a 'Pearl Harbor'; the South Vietnamese government was intact and stronger; the armed forces were larger, more effective, and more confident . . . and the enemy forces . . . were much weaker."[86]

Robert Shaplen suggests that militarily the offensive was a failure because it did not bring about the downfall of the Saigon regime, which is what the NLF and DRV had hoped for. But there were unanticipated benefits: the partial bombing halt of North Vietnam and the beginning of peace talks; then a full bombing halt in November and "the formal beginning of the period of 'fighting and negotiating at the same time.'" Shaplen reports that at least one American commander had anticipated the offensive. General Frederick

Weyand, who commanded the region around Saigon, cabled his unit commanders to be on guard against the possibility of "the enemy . . . deliberately violat[ing] the truce by attacking friendly installations during the night of January 29 or during the early morning hours of 30 January." Shaplen suggests that because NLF forces "were able to infiltrate so many men and weapons into [Saigon] . . . showed that an effective underground was in existence in the city."[87]

Leslie Gelb, director of *The Pentagon Papers* historians, states that the Tet Offensive finally broke public support for Johnson's policy of outlasting the NLF and DRV by choosing the "prolonged limited war." Thus began Nixon's updated "Vietnamization" policy (from 1946 to 1954 the French used this policy): the gradual phasing out of American combat forces "slowly enough to assuage American political opinion."[88]

The key incident of Tet was the battle for control of the old imperial capital city of Hué. In that battle some 10,000 soldiers and civilians died, and whole sections of the city were leveled by North Vietnamese rockets and American tanks, artillery, and bombing.

Shaplen describes the destruction he witnessed in Hué:

> I went to Hué and nothing I had seen during the Second World War . . . during the Korean War, and in Vietnam during the Indochina War or since 1965 was as terrible, in point of destruction and despair, as what I had witnessed. . . . Much of the city was in complete ruins. There were ninety thousand refugees receiving aid. . . . *Nearly four thousand civilians were killed in Hué . . . and most of them were the victims of American air and artillery attacks.*[90]

And Frances FitzGerald states: "To many Americans . . . the Tet offensive appeared to complete the demoralization of the Saigon government and its supporters."[89]

The controversy that still exists today surrounds the alleged massacre of these civilians by NLF-DRV troops as they held on or fled from the city. Noam Chomsky and

Edward S. Herman state that the official Washington-Saigon versions of the alleged massacres came to light "coincident with the Nixon Administration's attempt to offset the effects of the October and November [1969] surge of organized peace activity and to counteract the exposure of the My Lai massacre."[91]

After the fighting had subsided in Hué, its police chief estimated that some 200 people had been killed by the NLF-DRV forces, while a mass grave containing some 300 people was said to have been found by the mayor. But during the fall of 1969, some nineteen months later, a "captured document," which had been lost in the official files, came to light, stating that the enemy "allegedly boasts of 2748 persons having been 'eliminated' during the campaign." Few reporters questioned the document, or the long time lapse, and believed the official story that the "'Front and the North Vietnamese forces murdered some three thousand civilians' in their month of terror at Hué." This figure was inflated to 5,700 civilians by Robert Thompson, the British adviser to Diem and successive Saigon regimes.[92]

Chomsky and Herman cite the research of D. Gareth Porter, co-director of the Indochina Resource Center, who carefully investigated the incident and the "mysterious 'captured document.'" Among the contradictions raised: the 2,748 figure clearly included military deaths and injuries; the claim the NLF had blacklists for execution was directly contradicted by Hué's chief of secret police; and "no captured document has yet been produced which suggests that the NLF and DRV had any intention of massacring either civilians or even the established leaders of Hué."[93]

The proof for the mass graves came after the fact, and all from official sources. Chomsky and Herman argue that many civilians were killed when U.S. and South Vietnamese forces recaptured the city. Townsend Hoopes, a Department of Defense official with access to information, states that about 80 percent of the buildings in Hué were destroyed, and "in the smashed ruins lay 2,000 dead civilians." According to NLF-DRV sources, some civilians were buried in mass graves alongside their own soldiers, and many were bulldozed into graves by returning U.S.–South Vietnamese forces.[94]

Independent journalists were not allowed to witness the grave openings and despite numerous requests were unable to locate them. Chomsky and Herman state:

Perhaps the only Western physician to examine the graves, the Canadian Dr. Alje Vennema, found that the number of victims in the grave sites he examined were inflated by over sevenfold ... that most of them had wounds and appeared to be victims of the fighting, and that most of the bodies he saw were clothed in military uniforms.

They contend that little concern has been given to the possibility that the victims may have been killed by the returning South Vietnamese and U.S. forces. They cite Italian journalist Oriana Fallaci, quoting a French priest from Hué, who estimated about 1,100 students, university teachers, intellectuals, and religious people who had never hidden their support for the NLF had been killed after the South Vietnamese troops and U.S. Marines returned and took over the city again.[95]

The hysteria and public-relations effort behind the so-called Hué massacre served a vital purpose: It obscured actual massacres that had been going on for some fifteen months prior to the release of the captured document. This was the CIA-sponsored "Phoenix" program, which was begun in July 1968 and later revealed in congressional hearings. The program, which has been critically analyzed by Michael Klare, of the Institute for Policy Studies, was described by U.S. officials as "a systematic effort at intelligence coordination and exploitation." Small-scale raids were made into NLF or "contested" areas to "seize or eliminate persons who have been identified ... as VCI [Viet Cong Infrastructure] agents."

FitzGerald states that the "Phoenix" program, which would serve as a model for "Vietnamization,"

> succeeded in fashioning much the same instrument for civilian terror that the Diemist laws . . . had created in 1957–1958. The only difference was that . . . the terror was a great deal more widespread. . . . It gave the GVN, and . . . American troops as well, license and justification for the arrest, torture, or killing of anyone in the country.[96]

William Colby, former director of the CIA and director of the "Phoenix" program, testified that by 1969 "a total of 19,534 suspected . . . agents had been 'neutralized'—of this number 6,187 had been killed, 8,515 arrested, and 4,832 persuaded to join the Saigon side." Klare concludes that 20,587 had been killed by May 1971. Colby acknowledged that "'occasional abuses' . . . had occurred." The use of torture as a method of "persuasion" was verified by two former U.S. military-intelligence agents in congressional testimony. They testified that Vietnamese "were indiscriminately rounded up, tortured, and murdered by Americans in the effort to eliminate Vietcong cadres [NLF officials]."[97] Another former agent, K. Barton Osborn, testified that he "never knew an individual to be detained as a VC suspect who ever lived through an interrogation in a year and a half, and that included quite a number of individuals."[98]

Operation "Speedy Express," another pacification program, also contributed to massive civilian casualties. In late 1968 the U.S. Ninth Infantry Division launched an "accelerated pacification program" to place the Mekong Delta province of Kien Hoa back under Saigon's "control." Kevin P. Buckley of *Newsweek* reported on the operation:

> All the evidence I gathered pointed to a clear conclusion: a staggering number of noncombatant civilians—perhaps as many as 5,000 according to one official—were killed by U.S. firepower to "pacify" Kien Hoa. The death toll there made the My Lai massacre look trifling by comparison. . . .

The people who still live in pacified Kien Hoa all have vivid recollections of the devastation that American firepower brought to their lives in early 1969. Virtually every person to whom I spoke had suffered in some way. . . .

One old man summed up all the stories: "The Americans killed some VC but only a small number. But of civilians, there were a large number killed."[99]

THE AIR WAR

Facts about the air war during the Johnson and Nixon Administrations reveal not only awesome statistics of death and destruction but also alarming insights about the nature of the high-level government decision-making processes that called for that destruction. Chomsky cites Department of Defense data revealing that, in the period from 1965 to 1969, the U.S. dropped about 4.5 million tons of bombs on Vietnam, "about 500 pounds . . . for every man, woman and child in Vietnam. The total of 'ordinance expended' is more than doubled when ground and naval attacks are taken into account."[100] He makes a vital point often ignored in the bombing discussions: There were worldwide protests against the well-publicized bombing attacks upon the DRV, while more extensive, massive attacks on South Vietnam went relatively unnoticed. Americans knew "virtually nothing" about this bombing.[101]

A refugee report covering the period from 1965 through 1972 in South Vietnam listed 10,105,400 civilian refugees and 1,350,000 civilian war casualties (including 415,000 dead, 826,000 orphans, 80,000 civilian amputees, 103,000 war widows, and 40,000 blind civilians). The majority of these civilian casualties were attributed to U.S. and South Vietnamese fire power. During 1972 up to one-third of civilian war casualties were females 13 years of age or older, and up to one-fourth were children 12 years of age and younger. More than 50 percent of civilian war casualties admitted to hospitals were children.[102]

The bombing was defended continually by Presidents Johnson and Nixon and their advisers as precise and restrained, aimed only at military targets. But Neil Sheehan, former New York *Times* correspondent in Vietnam argues:

> There can be no doubt that ... Nixon and ... Johnson ... have used air power with the knowledge that this weapon exacts a terrifying price from the civilian population. ... The record shows that neither President acted in ignorance. During the air war against North Vietnam from 1965 to 1968, the Johnson Administration insisted in public that planes bombed only military targets ... with surgical-like precision.[103]

Sheehan further points out that during 1968 and 1969, the years of most intense fighting, the U.S. dropped almost 1 million tons of ordnance per year on South Vietnam, five times the maximum annual tonnage dropped on the DRV.[104]

The escalated bombing policy by the U.S. was always explained in terms of military necessities: cutting supply lines, destroying military related industry, and preventing enemy build-ups. Privately, however, in March 1966 the CIA issued a report recommending the need to direct the bombing against "the will of the regime as a target system." The report lamented that "75 percent of the nation's [North Vietnam] population ... had been effectively insulated from air attack." And further, it noted: "The policy decision to avoid suburban casualties to the extent possible has proved to be a major restraint."[105]

That restraint was being eroded from a variety of sources, because in January 1967, the CIA reported civilian casualties made up 80 percent of the total.[106]

In August 1967, at a congressional hearing of the Senate Armed Services Committee, Chairman John Stennis said to Admiral U.S. Grant Sharp, Commander in Chief of the U.S. Forces in the Pacific: "I want to leave with you some discretion about how far you go in bringing out the specific targets, because *if you are planning to bomb a place, I don't want to know about it frankly*" [emphasis added].[107] The whittling of restraints was clearly evident in a later exchange at the same hearings:

Senator Thurmond: Is there any reason why, if we want to win over North Vietnam, we can't put them on notice that we are going to bomb them and bomb them if necessary to bring this war to a close? That is what we did in Germany, wasn't it?

Admiral Sharp: I think that would probably be one thing that would bring it to the end.

Senator Thurmond: That would bring it to an end, wouldn't it?

Admiral Sharp: Yes, sir; one of the things we have to do to bring this war to an end is to demonstrate to the VC and the North Vietnamese beyond a shadow of a doubt that we are going to keep it up.

Senator Thurmond: That we have the will to win; we have the power to win; and that we are going to put the pressure on them until we do win.

Admiral Sharp: That is correct.

Senator Thurmond: And not have any letup *and not have any restraint merely because a few civilians near military targets clamor about bombing* [emphasis added].

We could put them on notice to move the civilians, couldn't we, out of any areas we were going to bomb, if necessary?

Admiral Sharp: We could.

Senator Thurmond: Although I don't think we did that in World War II.

Admiral Sharp: I don't think we did, either.

Senator Thurmond: We just said we were going to win and we took the steps to win. We can do it here if we have the will to do it.

But if we are going to listen to world opinion or Communist propaganda or State Department propaganda, then we won't win.[108]

Chairman Stennis closed that day's hearing by saying to Admiral Sharp: "Your testimony makes any thought of stopping the bombing unthinkable. That, in substance, is all I am going to say at this time to the news media."[110]

About the time of these hearings, Congressman Gerald Ford, then Minority Leader in the House, made a speech in Congress indicating his frustration over bombing restraints.

"Most Americans wonder why North Vietnam has not been totally destroyed. They remember what conventional bombing did to Tokyo and Berlin, to London and Warsaw. They wonder what can be left in North Vietnam worth bombing." Ford added, "Mr. Speaker, we are still pulling our best punch in North Vietnam."[109] Our "best punch" in Vietnam resulted in an increase from 650,000 tons of ground and air munitions used in 1965 to 2,883,000 tons of explosives dropped in 1968.[111]

A week after the hearings, General Earle G. Wheeler, Chairman of the Joint Chiefs of Staff, testified before the same committee. He seemed to be critical of allowing moral considerations to interfere with bombing plans, observing: "We are taking moral considerations into account in a very major way in waging this war, something we did not do, by the way, in World War II, where we had no compunctions at all about attacking targets in heavily populated areas."[112] However, it was the fear of international and domestic reaction, not moral considerations, that was the restraining force on U.S. war planners.[113]

A reading of the transcripts of these hearings leaves an impression that the military had their hands firmly tied by bombing restrictions, but nevertheless, while it is true that some restraints were put on the military, the collective record of U.S. military conduct in Vietnam indicates repeated violations of the minimum standards of constraints set by the Hague Convention of 1907, the Geneva Conventions of 1929 and 1949, and the "Nuremberg Principles" of International Law of 1950.

Since most of the brutal treatment of North Vietnamese and Viet Cong prisoners was carried out by the South Vietnamese, U.S. conduct was frequently exempt from criticism. However, Article 12 of the Geneva Convention of 1949 clearly states that those who have taken prisoners bear responsibility for the treatment given to them by those in whose custody the prisoners are placed.[114]

News dispatches from Vietnam during the middle 1960s

period of escalation bear grim testimony to these violations of international agreements on the rules of warfare. From an article by Desmond Smith in *The Nation*:

"Don't film," said the young lieutenant, with a smile. . . .
The lieutenant had been referring to the scene before us: A trooper was spraying insect repellent on a human ear. . . . "No, sir," I said, "we won't film that."
But I was curious to know more about this ear fetish. . . . So I walked out of the coconut grove and across the paddy dike. There I saw my first atrocity. His head slumped against the bank, a look of agony frozen beneath the shock of black hair. Both ears had been severed at the roots so that all that remained were two bloody circles about the size of 50¢ pieces. . . . He didn't look to have been more than 15. . . . I remember thinking that this was the first time I'd ever seen the face of the enemy, and it was just a kid.[115]

From the St. Louis *Post-Dispatch*:

Senator Stephen M. Young, D-Ohio, said today the South Vietnamese are executing many prisoners of war turned over to them by American fighting forces. Young said that "in the name of humanity and decency" [the United States] should stop transferring Viet Cong prisoners to South Vietnamese units. . . .
"Probably more of these prisoners are executed than are permitted to survive," he told the Senate.
At the same time, Young said, the conscience of the world would find it revolting if North Vietnam tried and executed American airmen held prisoner there.[116]

From the New York *Times:*

The United States is in the unhappy position of asking humane treatment for American prisoners of Communists while it has declined to guarantee similar treatment to Vietcong taken prisoners by American ground combat units.
Such prisoners, after a preliminary interrogation, are handed over to the Vietnamese authorities by whom of course they can be and frequently are subjected to brutality.[117]

Article 27 of the Geneva Convention of 1949 relative to the protection of civilians states in part: "Protected persons are entitled, in all circumstances, to respect for their persons, their honour, their family rights, their religious convictions and practices, and their manners and customs. They shall at all times be humanely treated, and shall be protected especially against all acts of violence or threats thereof."[118] Again, we have the testimony of the news dispatches. From the New York *Times:*

Vietcong casualty figures have always been difficult to pinpoint. As the Communists withdrew from Quangngai last Monday, United States jet bombers pounded the hills into which they were headed.

Many Vietnamese—one estimate was as high as 500—were killed by the strikes. The American contention is that they were Vietcong soldiers. But three out of four patients seeking treatment in a Vietnamese hospital afterward for burns from napalm, or jellied gasoline, were village women.[119]

From *The Evening Star* (Washington):

As the situation grows worse in Binh Dinh, air strikes are flown over populated areas.

A U.S. pilot back from a raid said: "I killed 40 Viet Cong today. That's the number they told me were in the village, anyway, and I leveled it."[120]

From the Cleveland *Plain Dealer* (excerpted from Sgt. Dennis Pena's letter to his parents):

What I didn't like was when we burned the village down. The women and kids were crying and begging you not to burn them down. A lot of them stay inside and you have to drag them out.

Ma, that's not good to see. I look back at what was once a village and the people crying, but as the sergeant told me, that's war. I guess he was right.[121]

After compiling 362 pages of such published reports of the behavior of American military personnel in Vietnam, the research team commissioned by Clergy and Laymen Concerned About Vietnam concluded: "There is a legal case to be made against our actions in Vietnam and it is, we believe, a devastating one. . . . In instance after instance the United

States has far exceeded the bounds of what is morally permissible in Vietnam."[122]

The forced relocations—and thus the urbanization of South Vietnam's previously rural population—caused by the massive bombing campaign were advocated by former Harvard professor and DOD adviser Samuel Huntington. Huntington's views reflected the high-level government thinking behind the bombing policy and were considered to be a possible answer to "wars of national liberation." He termed the U.S. policy "forced draft urbanization and modernization," which would displace the rural population (the base of the NLF's strength) and referred to the "direct application of mechanical and conventional power," which would take place on such a "scale as to produce a massive migration from countryside to city." However, this kind of genocidal policy would be prohibited under the guidelines set by the Nuremberg War Crimes Tribunal.[123]

Orville and Jonathan Schell, correspondents in Quang Ngai province during this period, saw first-hand the results of this policy. Jonathan Schell quoted an American Army officer: "Who has made this new policy? The Americans never try to protect a village. Just one V.C.—*just one*—can enter any village with a machine gun and the people are helpless against him. What can they do? Nothing. He shoots, and then their village is bombed."[124]

Another aspect of the air war was the defoliation campaign aimed at the ecological and agricultural bases of rural South Vietnam. Forest cover was defoliated so that NLF guerrillas could be more easily spotted from the air and bombed; and crops were destroyed to deny food to the guerrillas. By 1971 some 100 million pounds of herbicides had been sprayed on South Vietnam, covering almost 6 million acres. Approximately 35 percent of the tropical hardwood forests had been sprayed, thus destroying enough "merchandisable timber . . . to supply the country's domestic needs for about 30 years." In addition, about 50 percent of the coastal mangrove forests had been destroyed.[125]

The defoliation program had its major impact upon the already devastated rural population. The Herbicides Assessment Commission of the Association for the Advancement of Science found that the food destroyed would have fed about 600,000 people for a year. It discovered a "suggestive correlation" between periods of peak defoliation and an increase in stillbirths and birth deformities. And it was estimated that at least 12 million bomb craters had been created in South Vietnam, making some areas into "moonscapes," while creating stagnant water-havens for malarial mosquitoes.[126]

Despite this massive destruction, it was becoming apparent to some policy-makers as early as 1966 that U.S. aims were not being met by the existing tactics. This rising concern within the inner councils was debated strictly on pragmatic grounds; at no time did the destruction of Vietnamese life and culture interfere with the technical decisions. While Defense Secretary McNamara evidently had some "private" doubts about the success of the bombing campaign over North Vietnam, no doubts seem to have been voiced about the larger and more destructive bombing of South Vietnam. However, when professors George Kistiakowsky of Harvard and Jerrold Zacharias of M.I.T. suggested that he "convene a group of academic scientists" under the aegis of the Jason Division to examine the air war against the North and "investigate possible alternatives to the bombing strategy," he agreed.[127]

The Jason Division of the Institute for Defense Analysis, a group of 47 university scientists who worked on projects for the Department of Defense in their spare time, met during the summer of 1966. Their report concluded: "The U.S. bombing of North Vietnam had had no measurable direct effect on Hanoi's ability to mount and support military operations in the South at the current level"; and "no conceivable intensification of the bombing campaign could be expected to reduce Hanoi's ability to continue its logistical support of the guerrillas in the South." As an alternative it suggested developing an antipersonnel mine barrier across the demilitarized zone (DMZ) with an air-supported anti-truck system that would use electronic detection devices to direct air strikes. McNamara moved quickly to implement the recommendation, and work was begun on the barrier, although it was eventually abandoned by the Department of Defense because of its high cost. However, the system *was* used in Laos.[128]

Despite the recommendations of the Jason report in 1966, bombing continued, and not until the Tet Offensive in February 1968 would another serious investigation of air-war tactics be considered.

The Pentagon Papers state that the lesson of the Tet Offensive "should have been unmistakenly clear." The attempt to stop the flow of men and matériel from the DRV to the South had failed. "It was now clear that bombing alone could not prevent the communists from amassing the matériel, and infiltrating the manpower necessary to conduct massive operations if they chose."[129] After Tet, in February 1968, both McNamara and Johnson asked for a review of American policy and tactics. Johnson asked incoming Secretary of Defense, Clark Clifford, to review U.S. involvement; it would be called the "A to Z policy review" or the "Clifford group review," and its members included McNamara, General Maxwell Taylor, Paul Nitze of DOD, Nicholas Katzenbach of the State Department, Walt Rostow and Richard Helms of the CIA.[130] One of the papers they issued indicated that the CIA forecasts revealed little if any chance that intensified bombing would "break the will" of the DRV leaders, even with a "protracted bombing campaign aimed at population centers." Pragmatic concern was voiced that "deliberate attacks on population centers . . . would further alienate domestic and foreign sentiment and might well lose the support of those European countries which now support our effort."[131]

It was Clifford who supposedly suggested to Johnson the idea of cutting back the bombing of North Vietnam to the panhandle (below the 20th parallel). Dean Rusk noted that weather conditions in the Hanoi-Haiphong area would hamper bombing there in the coming months, and the curtailment would not "constitute a serious degradation of our military position."[132] The Clifford group rejected the Joint Chiefs' calls for more bombing and gave Johnson more of the same advice: hold to the strategy with a possibility of negotiations.

The Clifford review evidently was unsatisfactory to Johnson, and he called yet another group together for consultation on the war. Included among this group, known as the "Senior Informal Advisory Group," were Dean Acheson, former Secretary of State under Truman; Arthur Dean, New York lawyer and chief U.S. negotiator in Korea; General Matthew B. Ridgeway, former U.N. commander in Korea; Cyrus Vance, former Deputy Defense Secretary; McGeorge Bundy, president of the Ford Foundation and former National Security adviser to Presidents Kennedy and Johnson; and C. Douglas Dillon, former Treasury Secretary.[133] Eight of the nine men had been prominent hawks on the war, with one, Under-Secretary of State George Ball, characterized by *The Pentagon Papers* as a dove and "dissenter." However, Ball had been a member of the very policy-making bodies planning and executing the air war and other strategies, and his position might better be characterized as "mildly hawkish" in contrast to his colleagues.[134]

After three briefings by various Administration officials and advisers, the group told Johnson that continued escalation of the war could not work, that the United States should forget about a military solution in Vietnam and "intensify efforts to seek a political solution at the negotiation table." Johnson took their advice and began to move toward a political settlement, beginning with the announcement that General Westmoreland would be replaced as Commander in Vietnam.

In his famous speech of March 31, 1968, Johnson announced a "partial" bombing halt of North Vietnam and made a plea for negotiations. He also announced that he would not seek reelection in the fall.[135] The bombing would be restricted below the 20th parallel, but it actually meant a concentration of effort in that region and throughout South Vietnam, with "almost no reduction in total volume."[136] The intensity of the air war in affected areas would actually worsen. Johnson's gesture, however, led to other developments, for on April 3, the DRV agreed to the opening of the Paris Peace Conference, and the discussions commenced on May 10.

On October 31, Johnson announced a complete bombing halt over North Vietnam. This reportedly had been urged by Clifford, Ambassador Averell Harriman, and Cyrus Vance. But as with the earlier halt, the devastation over Vietnam had not ended; it had merely followed the March 31 pattern. "It would have been more accurate to say that in October, the bombing effort was also geographically rearranged, and was, again, intensified. The planes released from . . . North Vietnam were shifted to Laotian targets."[137] The New York *Times* reported that the military had plans to use the planes freed from the bombing of North Vietnam "for increased air strikes . . . in the south."[138]

Paul Sweezy, Leo Huberman, and Harry Magdoff, editors of the *Monthly Review*, place Johnson's decision to accept the advice of the elder statesmen, his call for negotiations, the bombing halt, and his announced resignation from public life in a critical perspective:

With his Gallup poll rating at its lowest point since he became President, unable (in the words of James Reston) to "venture forth into any of the great cities of the U.S. without the risk of serious demonstrations against him," having (according to Evans and Novak) "reached a nadir of popular support unprecedented for White House incumbents in this century . . . ," Johnson decided to call it quits before he would be further humiliated by his own Party or by the electorate.[139]

Despite Johnson's narrow victory over Eugene McCarthy in the New Hampshire primary in March and Robert Kennedy's intention to seek the Democratic nomination, Sweezy, et al., suggest that the most important reason for Johnson's fall was that he was "so thoroughly discredited that even the hawks would find his leadership a possibly fatal liability." Johnson's speech was accompanied by a large increase in the size of the Saigon army and more of the best and most sophisticated weapons. This would allow the United States to go to Paris from "a position of strength." The negotiations, or "peace policy," was actually "a war policy in the hands of the defenders of the American Empire."[140]

NIXON'S "VIETNAMIZATION" PROGRAM

Nixon's "Vietnamization" program was an effort to prolong the war by withdrawing American ground troops while increasing the mechanical means of destruction—the electronic battlefield and air war. Frances FitzGerald states that Vietnamization to Nixon meant ". . . a policy of scaling down the participation of American ground troops while increasing every other form of military pressure on the enemy. His aim was still to force Hanoi to accept an American-supported government in Saigon, and his strategy was still that of attrition. In fact, his policy involved little more than a change of tactics—and a change that originated not with him but with President Johnson in the summer of 1968. . . . And it was the same strategy that led to the situation the United States took over [from the French] in 1954."[141]

Michael Klare notes the urgency with which these various Vietnamization efforts were pushed:

With rising domestic opposition . . . the Pentagon has come under increasing White House pressure to avoid costly ground engagements in order to reduce American casualty figures. . . . This strategy, sometimes summarized as "firepower, not manpower," has naturally presupposed the increased use of detection devices to locate "lucrative" targets.[142]

He summarizes the larger historical issues involved in this

tactical shift: "President Nixon has been searching for a formula which would permit the United States to survive a protracted war without loss of our Asian empire, and without incurring further upheavals at home."[143]

A necessary aspect of the Vietnamization program was extensive development of highly sophisticated and advanced techniques of warfare. These included air-dropping sensors along truck routes in Laos; relay aircraft in orbit, which received the transmission from the sensors, relaying them to a ground facility; and sensor-equipped helicopter gunships for nighttime duty, with detection devices for locating the "enemy" in any kind of weather.[144] Leonard Sullivan, Jr., head of Vietnam-oriented Defense Department research, writes:

These developments open up some very exciting horizons as to what we can do five or ten years from now [1968]: When one realizes that we can detect anything that perspires, moves, carries metal, makes a noise, or is hotter or colder than its surroundings, one begins to see the potential. . . . You begin to get a "Year 2000" vision of an electronic map with little lights that flash for different kinds of activity. This is what we require for this "porous" war, where the friendly and the enemy are all mixed together.[145]

One "advantage" of U.S. involvement in Vietnam was its usefulness as a testing ground for such exotic military hardware and as a workshop to experiment with counter-revolutionary tactics, both political and military. But while part of Nixon's Vietnamization had to do with automating warfare in order to reduce U.S. casualties and to allow for gradual withdrawal of our troops, the main thrust of his plan was a bludgeoning air offensive.

Nixon continued to resist negotiations in the early 1970s. Despite increasing antiwar demonstrations, increased opposition inside the military, and a rapidly deteriorating political and military situation in South Vietnam, the Nixon-Kissinger team chose an intensified air war over a political settlement. In July 1971 the Provisional Revolutionary

Government of Vietnam (PRG), formed in South Vietnam by the NLF and other nationalist groups in June 1969, proposed a seven-point peace plan. But Nixon's unwillingness to accept a coalition government in Saigon, his demand for a unilateral cease-fire from the PRG while U.S. troops remained in South Vietnam, and his refusal to set a specific date for U.S. withdrawal once again destroyed any possibility for a negotiated settlement.[146] Consistent with past U.S. policy dating back to 1964 (and well documented by *The Pentagon Papers*), Nixon refused to deal with the key problem: *who is to hold political power in South Vietnam.*

The Nixon Administration had continually claimed that the North Vietnamese were demanding control over South Vietnam. Seymour Hersh, a Pulitzer-prize-winning journalist, interviewed a North Vietnamese high official, Ha Van Lau, on this crucial charge. Ha Van Lau stated that the DRV would favor a coalition government in Saigon, representing members of the present regime, the PRG, and South Vietnamese not included in either group. Thieu would be unacceptable, but other South Vietnamese would be acceptable to the PRG and the North Vietnamese.[147]

Having rejected North Vietnam's peace proposals, Nixon blamed Hanoi and ordered the pounding of the Hanoi and Haiphong areas in the heaviest air raids of the war. Publicly the Administration explained the bombing in tactical terms: to prevent enemy build-ups and to cut supply routes. However, "many high-ranking civilian and military officials say privately that many of the targets being struck and the manner in which the raids are being carried out are new designs for optimum political and psychological impact on North Vietnam, as opposed to the maximum military impact."[148] This "bombing for psychological impact" policy explains the tremendous destruction of civilian populations around Hanoi and Haiphong. For two weeks, extending into the Christmas holidays, Nixon unleashed a greater tonnage in bombing Hanoi and Haiphong than Hitler's bombing of Britain from 1940 to 1945. Worldwide protest was registered over both the large number of civilians killed and the hospitals and other humanitarian buildings destroyed. In late December 1972 Nixon stopped the bombing.

PARIS PEACE AGREEMENTS

On January 27, 1973, representatives of the Government of the Democratic Republic of Vietnam (North Vietnam), the Provisional Revolutionary Government of the Republic of South Vietnam (the PRG), the United States Government, and the Government of the Republic of Vietnam (South Vietnam) signed the *Agreement on Ending the War and Restoring Peace in Vietnam.* The Peace Agreement recognized the Saigon regime (GVN) and the PRG as *co-equal* administrations in South Vietnam. The main features of the Agreement signed in Paris committed the United States and the other signatories to respect the independence, sovereignty, unity, and territorial integrity of Vietnam; called for prisoners of war to be exchanged; and declared an in-place cease-fire. Specifically, Article 2 required the United States to "stop all its military activities against the territory of the Democratic Republic of Vietnam by ground, air and naval forces, wherever they may be based, and end the mining of the territorial waters, ports, harbors and waterways of the Democratic Republic of Vietnam." A key article—Article 4—stated further that "The United States will not continue its military involvement or intervene in the internal affairs of South Vietnam." It was enthusiastically received by the PRG and the North Vietnamese, who sensed victory through a political settlement, which had earlier been denied by the sabotage of the 1954 Geneva Agreements. However, the Thieu regime was extremely dissatisfied and signed the Agreement only reluctantly.[149]

The Agreement was successful in ending the U.S. bombing of Vietnam, in causing the withdrawal of American troops, and in bringing all American POW's home. But, as happened nineteen years earlier at the 1954 Geneva Conference, a U.S.-Saigon government alliance resulted in treaty subversion and forced a military settlement in place of a political one. From the start the Nixon Administration made it clear that it intended to ignore the PRG, and hence it violated the Agreement when it referred to "the three signers of the Agreement," excluding the PRG. Nixon stated: "The United States will continue to recognize the Government of the Republic of Vietnam as the sole legitimate government of South Vietnam."[150]

In violation of Article 4, the United States *continued* its involvement in the affairs of South Vietnam by sending General Thieu at least $813 million in military aid and planning an additional $1 billion in aid to enlarge Saigon's army.[151] By fiscal year 1975, the Administration was proposing $3.7 billion in aid for Indochina—69 percent ($2.513 billion) for military expenditures, 19 percent ($714.9 million) for war-related "economic assistance," 7 percent ($267.6 million) for reconstruction and development, and 5 percent ($172.4 million) for humanitarian purposes. The Administration's budget for aid to the rest of the world was $3.5 billion. The U.S. Government was proposing to spend 46.6 percent of its total aid abroad on only 0.8 percent of the world's population, and the bulk of this aid was to be military.[152]

Article 5 ordered the United States to totally withdraw all military and police advisers from South Vietnam, but the United States sent 8,000 "civilian" advisers and technicians to Thieu's regime.[153] Even the Pentagon admitted it had *increased* its advisement role for Department of Defense "civilians" from 818 on January 27, 1973, to 1,200 on December 31, 1973, and Department of Defense "civilian" contractors from 5,237 on January 27, 1973, to 5,500 on December 31, 1973.[154] The Nixon Administration claimed these Defense Department civilians and contractors were not engaged in giving military training or advice to the Vietnamese military or police units, and therefore it was not in violation of the Agreement. However, Lear Siegler, Inc., had a multimillion-dollar contract with the Defense Department for "Depot Maintenance and Training of VNAF [Vietnamese Air Force] personnel." Lear placed ads for jobs in Vietnam in more than twenty major American newspapers in the first four months following the Agreement; the jobs were to maintain the aircraft for Thieu's air force. Dozens of U.S. corporations, ranging from ITT to Motorola to Esso International (Exxon), were each doing more than a million dollars of defense-contract work in Vietnam as of April 1, 1973.[155]

While the United States was not to "impose any political tendency or personality on the South Vietnamese people" (Article 9), there was widespread agreement that U.S. aid was absolutely crucial to the Thieu regime's survival. One year after the peace agreement, U.S. taxpayers were paying 80 percent of the cost of maintaining the Saigon government.[156] Reports of corruption, mismanagement, black-marketing, and outright pilfering of the aid increased Thieu's unpopularity both in America and South Vietnam. According to the New York *Times*:

The U.S. remains the most vital lifeline to the military and economic stability of the [Thieu government]. . . . American economists in Saigon have no doubt that if the U.S. withdrew or if it further curtailed its aid, [Thieu's] already faltering economy would simply collapse. Nor could the military survive without American help.[157]

The Washington *Post* reported: "President Nixon asked Congress yesterday to authorize a $2.9 billion military and economic aid program [for Indochina] that pointedly omitted any reconstruction assistance for North Vietnam."[158] This was in violation of Article 21 which called for the United States to contribute to the postwar reconstruction of North Vietnam.

A frequently used rationale for aid to Vietnam was repeated by Graham Martin, U.S. Ambassador to Saigon:

"Our intention all along was to balance the aid given by the Soviet Union and the People's Republic of China to North Vietnam." In fact, the United States since 1966 through 1973 had spent 29 times as much as the U.S.S.R. and China combined (U.S. $107.10 billion, U.S.S.R. $2.57 billion, and China $1.08 billion.)[159]

Almost on the eve of the signing of the Agreement, January 22, 1973, President Thieu further limited the civil rights of Vietnamese citizens. His edict called for police and military forces "to shoot to kill all those who urge the people to demonstrate, and those who cause disorders or incite other persons to follow communism" and to "detain those persons who are neutralist and those persons who publicly side with the communists, and who are active politically."[160] The suppressive edict remained in force after the signing of the Agreement, which prohibited such infringements on personal liberties. Article 11 specifically insured "the democratic liberties of the people: personal freedom, freedom of speech, freedom of the press, freedom of meeting, freedom of organization, freedom of political activities, freedom of belief, freedom of movement, freedom of residence." The Washington *Post* reported that Saigon ". . . will not permit hundreds of thousands of refugees from Communist-held areas to return to their homes after the ceasefire takes effect and will punish them if they try."[161] The *Post* later reported that Saigon "has become more restrictive since the agreement took effect, rather than less."[162] The Thieu regime continued to violate the Agreement; it banned labor strikes and peace demonstrations, outlawed neutralization, and according to Amnesty International, imprisoned upwards of 100,000 civilians as political prisoners.

On November 1, 1973, Mr. Ho Ngoc Nhuan, deputy of the Saigon Assembly, pointed out that the Agreement, in essence, "wiped out the regime of the Republic of Viet Nam [the Saigon regime]. . . . It is also easy to understand why one side eagerly disseminated the entire Agreement by all means of communication and information it has while the other

side conceals, limits, and deforms the Agreement unceasing-
ly."[163] It is little wonder that Thieu from the start, with the
Nixon Administration's urging, wanted to sabotage the
Agreement.

A survey of the American press reports from Vietnam
during the first several weeks of the cease-fire indicate 30
eyewitness accounts by Western journalists of cease-fire
violations by Saigon forces.[164] No first-hand accounts of
PRG post-cease-fire violations were found in this same
period. Robert Shaplen filed a story from near Trang Bang,
South Vietnam, at 8 A.M. on January 28, 1973, the moment
the cease-fire went into effect. Just as he was listening to
President Nixon's peace proclamation being read over the
radio from Saigon, "the first of twenty-six five-hundred
pound bombs were dropped by South Vietnamese fighter-
bombers a hundred yards ahead of us."[165] Shortly after the
cease-fire began, the Joint Military Commission, the four-
power international inspection team, appealed specifically
for an end to "flights by bomber and fighter aircraft of all
types."[166] The Saigon regime had the only aircraft in South
Vietnam, and reporter Sylvan Fox of the New York *Times*
stated: "During the three-week old cease-fire, the South
Vietnamese Air Force has been flying 100 to 200 tactical air
strikes a day in South Vietnam."[167] Congressman Joseph
Addabbo of New York, in April 1973, asked Admiral
Thomas Moorer, chairman of the Joint Chiefs of Staff:
"Have the South Vietnamese been flying any sorties since the
cease-fire?" Admiral Moorer replied, "Yes, they have, within
South Vietnam."[168] Article 2 of the Agreement required the
United States "to stop all its military activities against
[North Vietnam] by ground, air and naval forces," yet the
officials of the State and Defense departments announced the
resumption of military reconnaissance flights over North
Vietnam.[169]

Saigon generals told U.S. Senate investigators that "there
had not been even one South Vietnamese Government
violation" of the cease-fire. However, information supplied

by the office of the U.S. Defense Attaché stated that the South Vietnamese Army "initiated several operations designed to expand areas of control to which the enemy reacted strongly," and that enemy activity "has been largely defensive or harassing in nature."[170]

The Washington *Post* summarized Thieu's reaction to the Paris Agreement:

> Thieu is continuing to run South Vietnam almost as if the Paris cease-fire agreement had never been signed, with the army and police as his principal instruments of statecraft. . . . In the words of one of his government officials, "Thieu has not yet made the fundamental decision to change from war to peace." South Vietnam remains under martial law with the army acting as a police force, court system, propaganda agent and civil administrator down to the lowest level of government. In short, the country remains, as a prominent government official put it, "a garrison state."[171]

The PRG and North Vietnam were once again forced into a military settlement, but no real attempt was made by the American media to assess who subverted the Agreement. Mass-media "objectivity" was best captured by Walter Cronkite when he summarized: "There never [had] really been a cease-fire. Almost from the very beginning both sides were accusing the other of truce violations."[172]

President Thieu's sabotage of the Agreement was completed with two swift events in late 1973 and early 1974. On December 28, 1973, Thieu announced there would be no general election in South Vietnam as called for by the Paris Agreement. The following week, on January 4, 1974, he said: "Pre-emptive actions of the South Vietnamese army had forestalled a Communist offensive, but the fight now had to be carried to zones occupied by the Vietcong under the cease-fire agreement, because the threat of an offensive still remained."[173] UPI reported: "The South Vietnam Government has announced its war planes are systematically bombing communist-held areas. . . . Although the Saigon government has admitted bombing Vietcong strongholds previously, it was the first open admission of systematic bombing across South Vietnam."[174]

By 1974 most of the American people had become thoroughly disenchanted of the war in Vietnam. The only remaining support for the war came from the Nixon Administration, and after Nixon's departure, the Ford Administration, with Secretary of State Henry Kissinger doggedly advising more aid for what some were suggesting had become an obsessional crusade for him. The Pentagon had continued to urge increased support for the rapidly deteriorating military situation. The beginning of the end, however, was signaled by congressional refusal to approve increases in funding. They had drawn the line at approximately 150 billion dollars.

In the spring of 1973 Congress passed antiwar legislation with a ban on funds for bombing or combat activity in Cambodia.[175] Until May 10, 1973, the House of Representatives had failed to pass any bill that would reduce or end U.S. military activity in Southeast Asia. Then in June 1973 a compromise bill allowed the bombing to be extended until August 15 of that year but prohibited any U.S. financing of military combat "in, or over, or from off the shores of North Vietnam, South Vietnam, Laos or Cambodia."[176] On November 7, both houses of Congress overrode President Nixon's veto, and the War Powers Act became law. This legislation requires a President to report to Congress within 48 hours of committing American forces to combat abroad, sets a 60-day deadline for such combat action, and within that period (a 30-day extension is permitted if the President deems it necessary for safe troop withdrawal) Congress can, by a simple majority vote, order immediate removal of U.S. forces (not subject to Presidential veto). In the last days of the Vietnam War, as Saigon and Phnom Penh were about to be liberated, President Ford was unsuccessful in his attempt to pass one last military-aid bill through Congress.

The end to the Vietnam War was swift. In March 1975

President Thieu ordered his troops to withdraw from the Northern provinces as a result of the defeat at Ban Me Thuot. The "strategic withdrawal" collapsed into a rout, however, and as ARVN soldiers fled, they frequently killed women and children for the scarce space on evacuating planes, ships, and motor vehicles.

In contrast to U.S. press reports of a North Vietnam final "offensive" in the South, Wilfred Burchett, an Australian correspondent who had covered the Vietnam War for two decades, wrote:

In 1975, there were practically no set battles, except for the brief one at Xuan Loc, guarding the approaches to Saigon. What happened was that guerrilla forces, which had been encircling towns and bases, in cooperation with people's organizations inside the towns, won over many soldiers within the enemy's armed forces. Popular uprisings and infiltrations were combined with the operations of the regular Liberation Armed Forces in a coordination of effort for which people and soldiers had all been preparing ever since the National Liberation Front was founded in December 1960.[177]

Burchett concluded his observations of this 30-year war with the insights that a careful, persistent reading of *The Pentagon Papers* secrets would have revealed to the public.

Military historians will study the phenomena of the defeat of the mightiest of the imperialist powers in Vietnam for decades to come. Unless they comprehend the nature of people's war, their conclusions will always be inaccurate. But to accept the validity of people's war is not possible for orthodox military analysts. The Westmorelands and Weyands of this world will go to their tombs saying: "If only our hands had not been tied . . . if only Congress had not stabbed us in the back. . . ."[178]

The Westmoreland-Weyand replay of history is one of many means for avoiding the lessons of our longest war. The lesson they learned—restraining the military's genocidal campaign against the Vietnamese people is what lost the war—is hopefully only a minority viewpoint. What remains to be seen, however, is how well we have learned that imposing our will by force in the internal affairs of another country is *not* our right. The rewriting of the Vietnam War by the textbooks examined here is not an encouraging sign that the lesson is being learned.

NOTES

1. Quoted in The Senator Gravel Edition, *The Pentagon Papers: The Defense Department History of United States Decisionmaking on Vietnam,* 5 vols. (Boston: Beacon Press, 1972), II:276. This edition hereafter will be cited as *The Pentagon Papers,* GE. For a detailed account of NSAM 273 and its affects on U.S. policy, see *The Pentagon Papers,* GE III, 17–32.

2. *The Pentagon Papers,* New York *Times* edition (New York: Bantam, 1971), pp. 234–35, 238–39. This edition hereafter will be cited as *The Pentagon Papers,* NYT ed. See also *The Pentagon Papers,* GE III, 606–10 for documentation of U.S. covert, provocative military activities.

3. *The Pentagon Papers,* GE II, 241.

4. Ibid., 275.

5. Ibid., III, 494–96.

6. Ibid., 46.

7. Ibid., II, 459.

8. Ibid., III, 511.

9. Ibid., 163.

10. Quoted in George McTurnan Kahin and John W. Lewis, *The United States in Vietnam* (New York: Dell, 1967), p. 401.

11. Franz Schurmann, Peter Dale Scott, and Reginald Zelnik, *The Politics of Escalation in Vietnam* (New York: Fawcett World Library, 1966), p. 16.

12. Ibid., p. 20. See also *The Pentagon Papers,* NYT ed., 261; and *The Pentagon Papers,* GE III, 83, 108, 270–71.

13. *The Pentagon Papers,* GE III, 34.

14. Noam Chomsky, "From Mad Jack to Mad Henry: The U.S. in Vietnam," *Vietnam Quarterly,* no. 1 (Winter 1976), pp. 26–27.

15. Quoted in Chomsky, p. 27.

16. New York *Times,* July 28, 1964.

17. Kahin and Lewis, pp. 163–64.

18. Ibid., p. 164n.

19. Allen Whiting, a key member of the U.S. intelligence and planning team, has provided additional information on the Pleiku attack. He writes that the U.S. bombing of North Vietnam on February 7, 1965, was "ostensibly in response to a guerrilla attack on American troops and aircraft at Pleiku." Whiting adds,

"Actually the raids were preplanned on the author's [Whiting] forecast that a Communist assault would be mounted against an American installation during the visit of McGeorge Bundy, the special assistant for National Security Affairs." (Allen Whiting, *Chinese Calculus of Deterence* (University of Michigan Press, 1975), pp. 178, 274n.

20. Quoted in the New York *Times*, February 25, 1965.

21. Kahin and Lewis, p. 171.

22. U.S. Department of State Bulletin (Washington, D.C.: GPO, 1965), p. 293. From August 1964 Bundy had insisted that negotiations could be considered: "After, *but only after*, we have [deleted] know that North Vietnamese are hurting and that the clear pattern of pressure had dispelled suspicions of our motives, we could then accept a conference broadened to include the Vietnam issue." See *The Pentagon Papers*, GE III, 535.

23. *The Pentagon Papers*, GE III, 438.

24. Ibid., GE V, 196.

25. Anthony Austin, *The President's War* (Philadelphia: J. B. Lippincott, 1971), p. 345.

26. Ralph Stavins, Richard Barnet, and Marcus G. Raskin, *Washington Plans An Aggressive War* (New York: Vintage Books, 1971), pp. 97-98.

27. *The Pentagon Papers*, GE III, 56-58, 83, 108-9, 182-91, 519-24, and 529. See also Stavins, et al., pp. 94-103; Schurmann, et al., pp. 35-43; *The Vietnam Hearings* (New York: Vintage, 1966), pp. 44-50 (exchange between Senator Fulbright and Secretary Rusk); Kahin and Lewis, pp. 156-59, 163, 182, 186, and 197; *The Pentagon Papers*, GE V, 320-41; and Eugene G. Windchy, *Tonkin Gulf* (New York: Doubleday, 1971).

28. Stavins, et al., p. 99.

29. Ibid., p. 126.

30. *The Pentagon Papers*, GE III, 598-601.

31. Ibid., GE II, 75.

32. *The Pentagon Papers*, NYT ed., p. 242.

33. *The Pentagon Papers*, GE III, 438.

34. Ibid., 473.

35. Ibid., GE IV, 297.

36. *The Pentagon Papers*, NYT ed., Chap. 6. See also *The Pentagon Papers*, GE III, 275-84 and 398-417.

37. *The Pentagon Papers*, GE III, 556-59. See pp. 270-71 and 286-90 for a brief summary of the background to the Pleiku incident.

38. Quoted in Stavins, et al., p. 110. See pp. 107-10 for a summary of the Sullivan Task Force report.

39. Ibid., p. 110.

40. Ibid., p. 111.

41. Ibid., pp. 125-26.

42. J. William Fulbright, *The Arrogance of Power* (New York: Random House, 1966), pp. 50-51.

43. *The Pentagon Papers*, GE III, 332-34.

44. Ibid., 391.

45. Ibid., GE IV, 49. See also Chomsky, *For Reasons of State* (New York: Random House, 1973), pp. 4, 5, and 70-87.

46. Bernard Fall, "Vietnam Blitz: A Report on the Impersonal War," *New Republic* 153 (October 9, 1965): 19.

47. New York *Times*, March 3, 1965.

48. Quoted in Harry S. Ashmore and William C. Baggs, *Mission to Hanoi* (New York: G. P. Putnam's Sons, Berkley Medallion Edition, 1968), p. 282; from Department of State Bulletin, May 10, 1965.

49. Eqbal Ahmad, "Revolutionary Warfare," in *Vietnam: History, Documents, and Opinions on a Major World Crisis*, ed. Marvin E. Gettleman (New York: Fawcett, 1965), p. 361.

50. David Kraslow and Stuart H. Loory, *The Secret Search for Peace in Vietnam* (New York: Vintage, 1968), p. 118.

51. Ibid.

52. Quoted in Schurmann, et al., p. 82.

53. *The Pentagon Papers*, GE III, 355.

54. Ibid., 357.

55. Ibid., 355.

56. Kraslow and Loory, pp. 120-21.

57. *The Pentagon Papers*, GE III, 273-74 and 354-56.

58. Ibid., 702-3.

59. Ibid., 417.

60. U.S. Cong., Senate, *Supplemental Foreign Assistance Fiscal Year 1966— Vietnam*, 89th Cong., 2nd sess., (Washington, D.C.: GPO, 1966), p. 122.

61. Kahin and Lewis, p. 432.

62. Ibid., pp. 212-13.

63. Quoted in the New York *Times*, December 12, 1965.

64. Kahin and Lewis, p. 214n.

65. New York *Times*, July 14, 1965.

66. Ibid., July 29, 1965.

67. Ibid., December 8, 1965.

68. Ibid., December 12, 1965.

69. Schurmann, et al., pp. 96-97, 105-6, and 108-9. See also Kraslow and Loory, pp. 129-35.

70. *The Pentagon Papers*, GE IV, 32–42. See also Ho Chi Minh's letter, New York *Times*, January 29, 1966.

71. Kahin and Lewis, p. 239n. See U.S. Cong., Senate, *U.S. Policy with Respect to Mainland China*, 89th Cong., 2nd sess., (Washington, D.C.: GPO, 1966), p. 349.

72. Kahin and Lewis, p. 242.

73. Frances FitzGerald, *Fire in the Lake: The Vietnamese and the Americans in Vietnam* (New York: Vintage, 1973), p. 444.

74. Ibid., pp. 444–45.

75. Ibid., pp. 445–47.

76. Ibid., pp. 448–49.

77. Ibid., p. 451.

78. Ibid., p. 449.

79. Robert Shaplen, *Time Out of Hand* (New York: Harper and Row, 1969), p. 388.

80. Kahin and Lewis, pp. 245–46.

81. Quoted in Kahin and Lewis, p. 246.

82. FitzGerald, pp. 86, 519–20, 524.

83. Ibid., pp. 524–25.

84. Ibid., pp. 525–26.

85. Ibid., pp. 521–22.

86. Quoted in Ibid., pp. 531–32.

87. Shaplen, p. 405.

88. Leslie Gelb, "Vietnam: Test of President's Distant War and Battle at Home," New York *Times*, May 1, 1975.

89. Shaplen, p. 412.

90. FitzGerald, pp. 529–30.

91. Noam Chomsky and Edward S. Herman, *Counter-Revolutionary Violence: Bloodbaths in Fact and Propaganda* (Andover, Mass.: Warner Modular Publications, 1973), p. 27.

92. Ibid.

93. Ibid., pp. 27–28.

94. Ibid., p. 28.

95. Ibid., pp. 28–29. See also Chomsky, *For Reasons of State*, p. 231.

96. FitzGerald, p. 550.

97. Quoted in Michael Klare, *War Without End* (New York: Random House, 1972), pp. 264–65.

98. Quoted in Chomsky and Herman, p. 23.

99. Kevin P. Buckley, "Pacification's Deadly Price," *Newsweek*, June 19, 1972, pp. 42–43.

100. Noam Chomsky, *At War With Asia* (New York: Pantheon Books, 1970), pp. 290-91.

101. Ibid., p. 99.

102. Cited in a summarizing report by The Indochina Resource Center, Washington, D.C. (From a report by Senator Edward Kennedy's Senate Subcommittee on Refugees, February 28, 1973), p. S3608.

103. Raphael Littauer and Norman Uphoff, eds., *The Air War in Indochina*, rev. ed. (Boston: Beacon Press, 1972), p. viii.

104. Ibid., p. 10.

105. *The Pentagon Papers*, GE IV, 71.

106. Ibid., p. 136.

107. *Air War Against North Vietnam*, Hearings before the Preparedness Investigating Subcommittee of the Committee on Armed Services U.S. Senate, 90th Cong., 1st sess., Part I (Washington, D.C.: GPO, 1967), p. 9.

108. Ibid., p. 58.

109. Ibid., pp. 70-71.

110. Ibid., p. 121.

111. Chomsky, "From Mad Jack to Mad Henry: The U.S. in Vietnam," p. 26.

112. *Air War Against North Vietnam*, pt. 2, p. 149.

113. Ibid.

114. *In the Name of America*, Study commissioned by Clergy and Laymen Concerned About Vietnam (Annandale, Va.: The Turnpike Press, 1968), p. 37.

115. Desmond Smith, "There Must Have Been Easier Wars," *The Nation* 204 (June 12, 1967): 746-47.

116. Quoted in *In the Name of America*, p. 66.

117. New York *Times*, September 30, 1965.

118. Quoted in *In the Name of America*, p. 32.

119. New York *Times*, June 6, 1965.

120. Quoted in *In the Name of America*, pp. 105-6.

121. Quoted in Ibid., p. 140.

122. Ibid., pp. 1-2.

123. Quoted in Chomsky, *At War With Asia*, pp. 54-55.

124. Jonathon Schell, *The Military Half* (New York: Knopf, 1968), p. 165.

125. Littauer and Uphoff, p. 93.

126. Cited in Ibid., pp. 95-96.

127. Cited in Michael Klare, *War Without End* (New York: Random House, 1972), p. 181.

128. Ibid., pp. 182-85.

129. *The Pentagon Papers,* GE IV, 235.

130. Ibid., 239.

131. Ibid., 251.

132. Ibid., 259.

133. Ibid., 266-67.

134. Noam Chomsky, personal communication, May 1976.

135. *The Pentagon Papers,* GE IV, 266-69.

136. Littauer and Uphoff, p. 13.

137. Chomsky, *At War With Asia,* pp. 42-43.

138. Quoted in Ibid., p. 43.

139. Paul M. Sweezy, Leo Huberman, and Harry Magdoff, *Vietnam: The Endless War* (New York: Monthly Review Press, 1970), p. 111.

140. Ibid., pp. 112, 118.

141. FitzGerald, p. 539.

142. Klare, p. 202.

143. Ibid., pp. 363-64.

144. Ibid., pp. 185-86.

145. Quoted in Ibid., p. 209.

146. For an analysis of Nixon's response to the PRG seven-point peace plan, see "A New Peace Proposal?" by Edward F. Snyder, Friends Committee on National Legislation, 245 Second St. NE, Washington, D.C. 20002.

147. New York *Times,* March 29, 1972.

148. Washington *Post,* December 20, 1972.

149. *Viet-Nam: What Kind of Peace?* (Berkeley: Indochina Resource Center, 1973). This also includes the text of the 1954 *Geneva Agreements* and the Indochina peace proposals since 1969.

150. Quoted in the New York *Times,* January 25, 1973.

151. New York *Times,* January 6, 1974.

152. Cited in *Documenting the Post-War War* (Philadelphia: National Action/Research on the Military Industrial Complex, 1974), pp. xi-xii.

153. New York *Times,* December 7, 1973.

154. Cited in *Documenting the Post-War War,* p. 27.

155. Directorate for Information Operations Office of the Assistant Secretary of Defense (Comptroller), in "Contract Awards for FY 1972 and First Three Quarters of FY 1973 (through March, 1973) for Cambodia, Laos, Thailand and Vietnam."

156. *Documenting the Post-War War,* p. 210.

157. New York *Times,* August 19, 1973.

158. Washington *Post*, May 2, 1973.

159. *Congressional Record*, June 3, 1974, p. 17391.

160. Thieu edict published in Tin Sang (government newspaper), January 22, 1973.

161. Washington *Post*, January 25, 1973.

162. Ibid., March 1, 1973.

163. Ho Ngoc Nhuan, "Violations of the Peace Agreement in Viet Nam," November 1, 1973. Excerpts from this document were reprinted in *Vietnam Report*, no. 1 (January, 1974), published by the Association of Vietnamese Patriots in Canada.

164. *Documenting the Post-War War*, pp. 16-17. Eyewitness reports of bombing and shelling by Saigon troops in the first ten days following the cease-fire came from Bui Chi, Xom Suoi, Pleiku, Kontum, Phong An, Tay Ninh, Binh Tanh, Kien Hoa, Phuoc Tanh, Trang Bang, An Loi Tan, Phan Thiet, Binh Phu, and Hoa Long. The reports appeared in the Los Angeles *Times*, January 30 and February 1, 1973; the *Wall Street Journal*, January 29, 31, and February 6, 1973; the Baltimore *Sun*, January 31 and February 16, 1973; the New York *Times*, January 29, 30, February 24, and March 6, 1973; the Washington *Post*, January 29, February 6, 22, and March 11, 1973; and Associated Press, United Press International wire services, CBS News, *The New Yorker*, and *Newsweek*.

165. Robert Shaplen, "Letter from Vietnam," *The New Yorker*, vol. 49, no. 1 (February 24, 1973), p. 106.

166. New York *Times*, February 18, 1973.

167. Ibid.

168. U.S. Cong., House, *Defense Appropriations Hearings*, Part 1, 93rd Cong., 2nd sess. (Washington, D.C. GPO, 1974), p. 168.

169. Quoted in the New York *Times*, August 19, 1973.

170. U.S. Cong., Senate, Committee on Foreign Relations staff report, *Thailand, Laos, Cambodia and Vietnam: April 1973*, Richard Moose and James Lowenstein, 93rd Cong., 1st sess., June 11, 1973.

171. Washington *Post*, February 18, 1973.

172. *End of the Vietnam War*, Walter Cronkite, narrator, CBS News Special, April 29, 1975.

173. Quoted in the Washington *Post*, January 4, 1974.

174. UPI, from Saigon, January 10, 1974.

175. Washington *Post*, May 11, 1973.

176. Ibid., June 30, 1973.

177. *Guardian*, (New York), May 14, 1975.

178. Ibid.

7

Conclusion: The Social Function of Secondary History Textbooks

Textbooks offer an obvious means of realizing hegemony in education. By hegemony we refer specifically to the influence that dominant classes or groups exercise by virtue of their control of ideological institutions, such as schools, that shape perception on such vital issues as the Vietnam War. Through their pretensions of neutrality and objectivity and through their suppression of data and alternative views, textbooks further the hegemonic process by establishing the "parameters which define what is legitimate, reasonable, practical, good, true and beautiful."[1] Within history texts, for example, the omission of crucial facts and viewpoints limits profoundly the ways in which students come to view historical events. Further, through their one-dimensionality textbooks shield students from intellectual encounters with their world that would sharpen their critical abilities. Despite the disclaimers of those who make a false separation between the world of textbooks and schools, and the world of public issues such as the Vietnam War, there is in reality a vital connection between the two. Noam Chomsky has commented on this connection:

... as American technology is running amuck in Southeast Asia, a discussion of American schools can hardly avoid noting the fact that these schools are the first training ground for the troops that will enforce the muted, unending terror of the status quo of a projected American century; for the technicians who will be developing the means for extension of American power; for the intellectuals who can be counted on, in significant measure, to provide the ideological justification for this particular form of barbarism and to decry the irresponsibility and lack of sophistication of those who will find all of this intolerable and revolting.[2]

The treatment of the Vietnam War in American textbooks serves as one of the means by which schools perform their larger social functions. Their most basic function is to obtain an uncritical *acceptance* of the present society, thus hindering rational analyses of conflicts such as Vietnam. Martin Carnoy of the Center for Economic Studies, Stanford University, argues that schools thus serve as "colonialistic" institutions designed to maintain the capitalist class structure, allowing "powerful economic and social groups *acting in their common self-interest*" to "influence ... schooling to further their own ends." This hegemonic domination is "eminently reasonable" once one understands the class nature and control of American society and education.[3] Similarly, the textbook examination of the Vietnam War is eminently reasonable once we understand the role it plays in the larger social functions of schooling.

Jonathan Kozol, author of the prize-winning educational work, *Death at an Early Age*, argues:

The government is not in business to give voice to its disloyal opposition. ... School is in business to produce reliable people, manageable people, unprovocative people, people who can be relied upon to make the correct decisions, or else nominate and elect those who will make the correct decisions for them.[4]

The textbooks we examined rarely raise the disloyal and controversial questions necessary to understand the origins and nature of the Vietnam War. Even those textbook authors who are seemingly critical of America's role in the war question it only within a very narrow framework. They rarely raise a fundamental point about the larger purposes of the war, and hence rarely encourage students to attempt a truly critical examination of it.

In *Pedagogy of the Oppressed,* exiled Brazilian educator Paulo Freire discusses education within the context of domination to indoctrinate individuals into an unquestioning acceptance of social reality. While Freire bases his educational views on the assumption that all persons have the potential to look critically and creatively at their world and can learn to comprehend and change oppressive conditions, he is nonetheless acutely sensitive to the manipulation of the educational process in order to maintain the hegemonic power of the dominant class.[5] The textbook authors are aiding this indoctrination. They are prime examples of what Paul Baran called the "intellect worker," which he defines as "the faithful servant, the agent, the functionary, and the spokesman for the capitalist system. Typically, he takes the existing order of things for granted and questions the prevailing state of affairs solely within the limited area of his immediate occupation."[6] The authors of these textbooks have taken this society and the official U.S. position on the war for granted; it has been assumed, not rationally investigated. They have not examined the fundamental nature of the war, nor the social, economic, and political contradictions that brought it about.

It is not surprising that textbooks have served this role, in that they must reinforce, not critically question, the larger political goals of the educational system. There is no conspiracy at work; it is merely that the texts must serve the more primary purpose—which is to have students support U.S. foreign policies rather than consider them critically and possibly reject them. It is also clear that the hegemonic parameters established by the texts exclude from inquiry any consideration that the liberation struggle of the Vietnamese was a justifiable one against a foreign invasion aided by native client forces and leaders. Such an interpretation is evasive, offering no more than a consolidated construct, a homogenous view of historical events. Rather than undertake the difficult task of self-criticism which might expose their underlying premises on American society, foreign policy and the Vietnam War to impart a comprehensive, honest picture of the conflict, the authors and publishers of these texts have adopted what Chomsky terms "a 'pragmatic attitude' . . . that is, an attitude that one must 'accept,' not critically analyze or struggle to change, the existing distribution of power, domestic or international, and the political realities that flow from it."[7]

The textbooks' examination of the Vietnam War is similar to the treatment of other vital issues in American history. Morgart and Mihalik, sociologists of education, have analyzed the role of social science and educational materials in the treatment of labor unions and the working class and conclude that in addition to the actual class-biased socialization of certain behavior for students, schooling also fosters a "cognitive socialization" regarding the prevailing ideological positions. Thus both the experience of schooling and the content of materials, such as these texts, allow teachers and students to avoid or obscure questions central to a critical understanding of American society and foreign policy. Morgart and Mihalik argue that what is at work in the schools is a narrowing of the field of investigation: "This regulation of ideas—which by the way needn't be an all or nothing kind of totalitarian regulation—can be affected by that which *is* learned and that which *is not* learned."[8]

The crucial issue here is the judgment students and teachers will make about the Vietnam War in American history. Chomsky has defined the educational import of this issue when he writes that the same forces who attempted imperial domination of Vietnam, and who "suffered a stunning defeat," will now attempt to explain this defeat to the American people, who are "a much less resilient enemy." He argues that "the prospects for success are much greater. The battleground is ideological, not military."[9] Our examination of these textbooks forces us to share his deep concern.

Chomsky states that the intelligentsia (the intellect workers) will play a key role in attempting to see that no "wrong lessons" are learned from the war or from the resistance to it. "It will be necessary to pursue the propaganda battle with vigor and enterprise to reestablish the basic principle that the use of force by the U.S. is legitimate, if only it can succeed."[10] Given the present analysis found in the textbooks, it is highly unlikely that in the near future textbook authors will seriously consider his conclusion on the purposes of the conflict. They "may concede the stupidity of American policy, and even its savagery, *but not the illegitimacy inherent in the entire enterprise.*"[11] From our investigation, we conclude that it would be extremely naive to expect this position to get much of a hearing in American schools. To pursue this line of reasoning would necessarily lead to a critical assessment of American domestic and foreign policy, and a reassessment of the basic purposes and functions of education itself.

The textbooks reveal the meager extent to which critical thinking emerges in historical material; to the extent that it does in schools, we must thank teachers who have gone far beyond the apologetic nature of these textbooks. The texts rationalize and affirm the official U.S. view, rarely placing the assembled facts in the context of a reasoned and rigorous examination. Their judgment on the war is invariably one of tactics, not of ends or purposes. As Noam Chomsky asks, "could we have won? Other questions might be imagined. Should we have won? Did we have a right to try? Would an American victory have been a tragedy of historic proportions? Were we engaged in criminal aggression?"[12] Such heretical thoughts have been obscured by these texts. Thus the educational dialogue on the war can continue in a technically "free" manner because the parameters of dialogue have been safely restricted.

The textbooks do not call into question any of the major premises of American foreign policy, premises that formed the foundation of the Vietnam War, that Chomsky argues are shared by both doves and hawks. What are these premises? "The U.S. government is honorable. It may make mistakes, but it does not commit crimes. It is continually deceived and often foolish . . . but it is never wicked. Crucially, it does not act on the basis of perceived self-interest of dominant groups, as other states do."[13] To expect schools to use materials that call into question the honor and veracity of U.S. relations with the rest of the world is asking much of education and textbooks. It is asking the schools to subvert their present function: to integrate students into the logic of the system.

Chomsky is correct: It would be foolish to expect the schools "to deal directly with contemporary events." He argues, however, that an effort could be made to analyze critically past imperialist efforts, such as the Philippines War (1898–1901), in order to better understand present deceptions.[14] It is not unreasonable to expect this critical examination to happen to some degree, but judging from the textbooks we examined, the extent to which it occurs is rare. Tragically, many teachers and students have examined such epic events in American history as the Vietnam War with little rational understanding of the root causes or its relevance to present U.S. actions, such as involvement in Third World liberation struggles in southern Africa, Latin America, and the Middle East.

Consider Chomsky's overall assessment of the war:

The American record . . . can be captured in three words: lawlessness, savagery, and stupidity—in that order. From the outset, it was understood, and explicitly affirmed . . . that the U.S. "intervention" in South Vietnam . . . was to be pursued in defiance of any legal barrier to the use of force in international affairs. . . . Lawlessness led to savagery, in the face of resistance to aggression. And in retrospect, the failure of the project may be attributed, in part, to stupidity.[15]

The bitter reality is that the texts we examined never consider that this assessment might be accurate, or *even that it is a position which could be investigated rationally and then rejected.* Those in dominant class positions in America, who were ultimately responsible for the invasion of Vietnam and the deception and contempt directed at the American people, will do all they can to frustrate such an investigation. They are well aware that such knowledge carries with it profound implications for public policy; that a critically informed understanding of the Vietnam War will undermine their hegemonic domination, particularly if students emerge from our schools with a healthy distrust of the government, its role in Vietnam, and present and future foreign adventures.

Generations of educators, many of them uncritical and seduced by the "Big Lie" of the dominant class, have labored to keep such a critical inquiry from the schools and the textbooks. The possibility of opening the debate on the Vietnam War in the schools rests not only with those who understand the real tragedy of Vietnam, but with those who are willing to fight for truthful history in the schools.

SOME FINAL THOUGHTS

When we began this project, we had no illusions of discovering any fundamental analysis of U.S. policy in Vietnam. We found instead that the basic purposes of U.S. policy were avoided, and thus the "critical" views that emerge do so within a carefully limited framework.

The twenty-eight textbooks present a political spectrum from the conservative-hawk position, which dominates the earlier texts (1961–68), to a middle of the road apologists' perspective, which dominates the later ones (1970–78). The conservative-hawk view is basically that of the U.S. standing firm against the Communists who were invading free South Vietnam. Reflecting the Cold War mentality of the 1950s, these texts often argue that the invasion was instigated and directed by the Chinese and the Russians. The later texts avoid this simplistic view; rather, they emphasize a new outside agitator, the North Vietnamese, with China and the Soviet Union now providing material aid and moral support. The conservative-hawk position parrots the then prevailing official view on the domino theory, while the later texts move away from this perspective, yet continue to avoid any possible suggestion that the domino theory was in fact simply a justification.

The middle of the road texts embrace the more sophisticated "Quagmire" thesis, in which the United States became involved out of honorable motives but became entangled in a war that could neither be understood nor won despite the best of intentions. The textbooks thus exclude, *even as a valid thesis for examination,* the position that the conflict was a logical extension of imperialist policies that first brought the United States to China, to the Philippines and Korea; that our efforts in Vietnam were simply a continuation of earlier French colonialism. The perspective of such historians as Gabriel Kolko, who argues that there is overwhelming evidence of "how devious, incorrigible, and beyond the pale of human values America's rulers were throughout this epic event in U.S. history,"[16] remains outside the limits of debate.

While the earlier texts view South Vietnam as a free nation under attack by the Communists, the later view freely admits the corrupt nature of the Diem family and successive regimes, but in a manner that shows no real insight, sheds no real light, on the fundamental causes of the conflict or of U.S. motives in supporting such regimes. The later texts reveal a pathetic tale of the kind-hearted but stumbling American giant who was trapped and manipulated by South Vietnamese allies, wishing to help but held back by the likes of Diem, Ky, and Thieu.

A consistent use of biased language describes NLF-DRV actions and motives, while U.S. premises and tactics are presented either in benevolent or technical-military terms. Thus the Viet Cong and the Communists terrorized the people to gain their support (although it is admitted in later texts that they had *some* support among the people because of the excesses of the Diem regime), while U.S. actions are framed in terms such as massive firepower, strategic hamlets, protective reaction, and "search and destroy" operations. Nowhere is it suggested that U.S. tactics, including defoliation, search and destroy missions, and civilian bombing raids, were inherently terroristic, clearly war crimes as defined by the Nuremberg Tribunal. Nowhere is it suggested that the Vietnamese who fought against the United States were principled and dedicated, as opposed to the officially supported parade of businessmen, generals, landlords, war profiteers, and pimps. There is no recognition of the view that in this war the United States might have been "the [enemy] of men who are just, smart, honest, courageous, and *correct*."[17]

Twenty-eight textbooks examined the most bitter conflict in recent American history without calling into question a single fundamental premise surrounding the conflict. The limited margin of debate and dissent was maintained, safe from attacks upon the honor and integrity of our leaders, or upon the nation itself. American high-school students, teachers, and parents could read these textbooks without *considering* the possibility that they lived in a nation that had committed the most blatant act of aggression since the Nazi invasions of World War II.

NOTES

1. Quoted in Robert Morgart and Gregory Mihalik, "On What Isn't Learned in School: School, Social Science and the Laying on of an Anti-Labor Ideology," American Educational Studies Association, New York, November 2, 1974, p.,11.

2. Noam Chomsky, "Thoughts on Intellectuals and the Schools," *Harvard Educational Review* 36, no. 4 (1966), p. 485.

3. Martin Carnoy, *Education as Cultural Imperialism* (New York: David McKay, 1974), pp. 13-24. Other recent critical analyses of American education include Samuel Bowles and Herbert Gintis, *Schooling in Capitalist America* (New York: Basic Books, 1976); Joel Spring, *Education and the Rise of the Corporate State* (Boston: Beacon Press, 1973); and Paul Violas, *The Training of the Urban Working Class* (Chicago: Rand McNally, 1978).

4. Jonathan Kozol, *The Night is Dark and I am Far from Home* (Boston: Houghton Mifflin, 1976), pp. 65-66.

5. Paulo Friere, *The Pedagogy of the Oppressed* (New York: Herder and Herder, 1970).

6. Paul Baran, "The Commitment of the Intellectual," in *The Longer View*, ed. John O'Neill (New York: Monthly Review Press, 1969), p. 5.

7. Chomsky, p. 489.

8. Morgart and Mihalik, p. 5.

9. Chomsky, "The Remaking of History, *Ramparts*, vol. 13, no. 10 (August/September 1975), p. 30.

10. Ibid.

11. Ibid.

12. Ibid., p. 31.

13. Ibid., p. 52.

14. Chomsky, "Thoughts on Intellectuals and the Schools," p. 489.

15. Chomsky, "The Remaking of History," p. 54.

16. Gabriel Kolko, "The American Goals in Vietnam," in *The Pentagon Papers: Critical Essays*, eds. Noam Chomsky and Howard Zinn, GE V, 14.

17. Carl Oglesby, "Vietnam Crucible: An Essay on the Meanings of the Cold War," in *Containment and Change*, Carl Oglesby and Richard Schaull (New York: Macmillan, 1967), p. 141.

Index

Index